SEX AND MARRIAGE IN ANCIENT IRELAND

SEX AND MARRIAGE
IN
ANCIENT IRELAND

PATRICK C. POWER

MERCIER PRESS

MERCIER PRESS
PO Box 5, 5 French Church Street, Cork
and
16 Hume Street, Dublin

Trade enquiries to CMD Distribution, 55a Spruce Avenue, Stillorgan Industrial Park, Blackrock, Dublin

© Patrick C. Power, 1976
This edition 1997

A CIP is available for this book from the British Library

ISBN 1 85635 062 2

10 9 8 7 6 5 4 3 2 1

FOR MY DAUGHTER ANN

Printed in Ireland by Colour Books Ltd.

CONTENTS

FOREWORD

THERE IS A GRADUAL TEARING away of the rather dishonest and prurient reticence which veiled subjects such as sex and marriage. There is a great curiosity abroad in Ireland today which seeks to see the past without preconceived ideas and to distrust the lopsided view of Ireland's story which often passed for history. This involved ignoring or covering up matters, such as those which are discussed here, in the name of modesty and decency. If it was modesty, it was dishonest; if it was decency, it was a sham. Women have demanded, and grasped, a new liberty.

Attitudes towards women range from the barbarous wife-beating one to the equal treatment of a woman by a man right through to such notions as the romantic one (the woman is a goddess!) and the Victorian attitude of the inherent purity and chastity of women, something which involves a total deprivation of a woman's zest for life. One will find that women were regarded in the laws of early Ireland with a humanity which is refreshing. Whatever happened sometimes in practice is another matter. At least the law was always on their side in a manner which was not the case so often in later Ireland.

I wish to thank my good friends the Librarians, Mrs K. Hayes of Waterford County Library, and Miss P. Fanning of Waterford City Library. Without the help and generosity of these ladies I could not have written very much. For a writer living in the countryside people such as they are invaluable friends and their aid is indispensable.

INTRODUCTION

IT IS BECOMING THE fashion nowadays to say that Ireland is part of the 'permissive society' which is found in North America and Western Europe. By 'permissive society' is meant more tolerance of human sexual desires and greater freedom in sexual expression than was the case hitherto. It is paradoxical that while sexual permissiveness increases, many of the small important freedoms of the individual are being filched by the modern state. This is happening in Ireland also. The enemies of sexual freedom would have us believe that somehow all of this is contrary to the traditions of Gaelic Ireland, which has been pictured as a land of saints and scholars and later as a land of pure-hearted Catholic martyrs.

One freedom that was sought but denied by the southern Irish state until 1996 was that of divorce. It had been allowed at first by the Irish Free State but in an excess of puritanical zeal it was forbidden on 11 February 1925. In the British-occupied part of Ireland divorce has been allowed because it was under English law. This created the farcical situation of the Roman Catholic Church giving annulments in their ecclesiastical courts – contrary to the law of the state in the south. When the partners remarried in church, they were bigamists in the eyes of the civil law. The increasing number of broken marriages eventually made it obvious that divorce should be permitted by the state. Of course the Roman Catholic Church totally disproves of all this.

Yet the southern Irish state had seen itself in the past as the heir, according to its protagonists, of ancient Gaelic Ireland. It will be clear from the evidence presented in this book that divorce was alway permitted in the ancient Gaelic Ireland under the brehon laws and that this did not come about here again until 1996.

Until recently reticence with regard to sexual matters was regarded as *de rigueur* in Ireland; in public, at any rate. Nowadays the newspapers, magazines, television and radio have altered all this. Frank and explicit discussion of the most intimate matters is now acceptable. Years ago such discussion was confined to the strong-holds of male society, the public houses, where the level of discussion was sometimes, to put it mildly, crude and low. Economic conditions had forced men to marry late in life and sex and marriage could become explosive subjects. Children were allowed to grow up with little or no knowledge of sex, except what they heard from one another. In schools and colleges any 'dirty' talk as conversation on these matters is sometimes termed, was severely punishable. This has also changed rapidly since the 1960s.

It is proposed to attempt to discuss in this book the position of sex and marriage in early Ireland. There is a large body of facts available on the subject but for some reason nobody has ever made any effort to write on them or to introduce them to the public. For the overwhelming majority of people in Ireland they are unexplored. One very interesting impression has been created by the teaching of Gaelic in the schools. This is the idea that the language itself is a kind of chaste linguistic system with nothing earthy or bawdy in it. With this false impression in mind no one can be surprised that more intimate and personal matters, such as sex and marriage, should be ignored because they were allowed to be unknown. The translators and adapters of early Irish tales are partly to blame. In the beginning of the twentieth century a Celtic twilight of warriors and heroes was drawn from the old literature and created in English. This twilight concealed the love-torn and the lusty men and women whose stories have been preserved for us. The ancient literature is certainly not an erotmaniac's paradise, as opponents of Gaelic liter-

10

ature in Irish schools endeavoured to prove in the early 1900s. It is, however, an earthy and natural expression of healthy people.

In this work, it is intended to make use of the laws of early Ireland, usually described as the brehon laws. These are a revelation for anyone thinking that the modern Irish attitudes to sexual and marital affairs are somehow that of the ancestors. Nothing could be further from the truth. In sober legal language the brehon laws legislated for Irish society in a manner which puts the most indulgent and humane legal system to shame. Since they were in force throughout the land until the twelfth century, they form a very important body of source material for this work.

Looking back to the 1920s it is a little strange that the first native government took over the full British system of law virtually without a single alteration. No attempt whatever was made to form a native system. When one looks at the declared aims of this and later governments to Gaelicise the country, one can only comment on the shallow hypocrisy of it all. Indeed a law forbidding divorce was passed by that first government and a kind of sub-Victorian state, in the most pejorative sense of the term, emerged to reach the dead years of the 1950s.

ANCIENT IRELAND
For the purposes of the present short study 'ancient Ireland' is understood to refer to the period from the dawn of history until the coming of the Normans in the twelfth century. Up to the introduction of Christianity in the fifth century there were no written records, apparently, or if there were, they have long since disappeared. In effect, therefore, we are speaking of an Ireland in bygone days where the Christian religion was accepted and where whatever pre-Christian religion in existence beforehand had given way to the new system of belief brought in from Europe. It should be mentioned that the references to pre-

11

Christian Ireland in the early records are highly suspect, to say the least of it. Since they are the only ones available, we must use them with caution.

Irish society in the period under discussion was certainly not a classless society. On the contrary, it was strictly divided into several distinct classes, as any human society must be in order to survive. There was the general division into the noble grades and the commoner grades. Irish law recognised three grades of kings; the *rí tuaithe* or king of a single *tuath*; the *ruireach* or overking, king of several *tuatha* and at the top the *rí ruireach* or *rí cóiced*, the king of the province. The king and the nobles were the rulers of the *tuath*. The commoners were distinct from the aforementioned by having a client-like relationship with someone of noble grade. However, the commoners had their legal rights and no one dare infringe them.[1]

The legal system of ancient Ireland is something totally different from what we know today. First of all it was customary law. It grew from the customs of the early Gaelic tribes and remained virtually immutable even until the seventeenth century when finally the last areas where it was still observed fell into the hands of the English. The most that the experts in this law could do was to comment on it. There was no concept, such as the State, which could require the obedience of the people to the law. The small government-unit – the *tuath* – was small enough to ensure that the force of tradition could claim respect for the old customs and the principal ones were enshrined in the ancient laws. The lawyers wrote down the statutes and commented on them. When a case arose, they consulted their texts and decided what the right course of action should be. The enforcing of their decision was the business of the kindred of the aggrieved party. There were no jails nor written contracts nor indentures. The long memory of the Irishman of that time was as good and as accurate as it is today; his dedication to the exact observance of ancient

12

law and custom was as total as a member of a closely knit community in a rural society can be.

To return to the class-society which was ruled by these ancient laws for a moment: each one had a 'price' fixed for him in the eyes of the laws. Generally speaking, if anyone committed a crime against another, the penalty was decided in accordance with the rank and worth of the plaintiff. Hence we come to what was called *enechlann* or honour-price. Any crime or misdemeanour could be termed an offence against a man's or a woman's honour and the penalty was calculated in accordance with its seriousness. There was another penalty called *díre* or *corp díre*, a term which may mean a form of atonement, something similar to the honour-price. The honour-price of a *rí* was seven *cumals* or female slaves, while his wife's was half this. The very serious crime of murder was in a special category of its own and for this the penalty was known as *éraic*. The penalty was not the barbarous one of legal murder, known as capital punishment, but a payment of seven *cumals* for every freeman, irrespective of rank. For bodily injuries a fraction of the *éraic* was obtainable by the injured man or woman. The interesting word 'blood-money' has been occasionally used to translate the term *éraic*, which actually means 'out-payment.'[2]

One's kindred were the enforcing authority of this law which is often called the 'brehon law' in English; one's importance and worth depended on status; the lawyers were specialists who interpreted and commented on the brehon laws. Against this background the reader must view the society in which sex and marriage is being discussed in this book.

ATTITUDES TO MAN–WOMAN RELATIONSHIPS

The brehon laws give a very interesting hint as to what the writers thought a man and woman should be ideally. In a short passage of bogus etymology, it is stated that the word *fer* (man) derives from the Latin word *virtus,* which means strength. Turning next to the word *ben* (woman), we are informed that it comes from the Latin term for goodness and the writer cites the word *benignitas* (kindness) as an example of what he had in mind. Strength from a man and kindness from a woman were, therefore, what was expected from the specialists who dealt with the ancient laws of Ireland.[3]

It should also be recalled that the highest honour-price for a *rí* was seven *cumals* – seven female slaves. The *cumal* was the highest unit of value known to the law. It does not have to mean that actual girls were exchanged in transactions but this must have been the case originally. One can gauge how the female slave was regarded by her value. She was equal to six *séts* normally, which were equal to three milch cows or six summer-heifers (i.e., dry or non-milk producing). In case any modern person considers this a matter of hilarity, it should be pointed out that in the totally non-urban and rural society known to the brehon laws the cow was indeed the queen of wealth and the standard of all monetary value.[4]

It has been stated by Professor Eoin MacNeill that the status of women in early Ireland was especially high when it is compared with what it was, for example, among the Romans. He thinks that this was due to the influence of the peoples who ruled Ireland before the Gaelic folk came, the folk who brought with them the basis of the brehon laws.[5] It should be noted that an invading force in these far-off times would consist of men without wives, to whom the wives of those they conquered fell as part of the booty. These women, reared in some liberty, would hardly agree to accepting a lower status than what they were accustomed to. One can subdue a man by threats of death or servitude, but one must come to terms with a woman, with whom one wishes to have a close relationship. No man can live forever on rape, especially with a free-minded and spirited woman.

It is worth looking at the story of Maeve, the Queen of Connacht which was written down in the eleventh century, although many elements of it go away back to much earlier times. She was the lady who is said to have led the famous cattle-foray from Connacht into Ulster to capture the Brown Bull of Cooley. Whether she is a mythical figure or not the picture we get of her must certainly be an accurate reflection of what a woman could set herself out to be in early Ireland. Maeve's husband arouses her anger when he states that she is worthwhile because of his status. She then goes on to prove that she has a status in her own right as good and even better than his. She does this in the following ways:

i) Maeve points out that she is the daughter of a king, the best of his four daughters. She then reminds her husband that she was also the best warrior of the four.

ii) She recounts how many fighting-men she has in her own right and how she has been made Queen of Connacht by her father. This she did not receive by means of her husband.

iii) Now comes something much more interesting than the foregoing. Maeve reminds her husband that it was she who selected him and that he attracted her by his three qualities – generosity, lack of fear and lack of jealousy. Her wish for a generous partner was prompted by her desire not to have him lose face by her great generosity. The same type of thing applied in the case of his fearlessness, because she was without fear. As to lack of jealousy, she explained that she was always wont to take one lover after the other and for this reason could not marry a jealous man.

One should note the 'liberated' attitudes, as the modern term has it, of the heroine of the ancient Irish people. She was her own person and was equal in status and importance to her husband. She claimed for herself and took all the liberties which most men always considered their own and then denied to their wives. Worse still, they have had their women schooled to regard such deprivation of liberties as some kind of womanly virtue.[6]

When speaking of Maeve and the Cattle-Raid of Cooley, we should refer to the *cess noínden*.[7] This has been explained in the saga as an illness which beset the men of Ulster in their hour of need and which incapacitated them from fighting. The term itself seems to mean 'children-pain', in other words, labour-pains. Much speculation has been made about this. It has been suggested, for example, that it is a remnant of a tradition about the existence of the couvade – the primitive custom of men suffering labour pains in sympathy with their wives. No hint of explanation is given in the ancient chronicles which come from the monasteries, where such customs as the couvade would hardly be expected to have been understood or tolerated. The story offered in explanation is, however, rather interesting. It is related that a Queen of Ulster, Macha, was put in the position of having to run a race against swift horses when she was in advanced pregnancy. She won the race but began labour immediately afterwards. In her agony she cursed the Ulstermen and said they would be attacked by the *cess noínden* when their need of vigour and mobility was greatest. It thus happened, according to the old saga, that the men of Ulster were incapacitated by this female problem when Maeve sallied into their province. Only the hero, Cuchulainn, who was not an Ulsterman, did not suffer from it and faced Maeve's hosts alone.

Cuchulainn had a peculiar gess or taboo. On the direst penalties each great man in ancient Ireland had to obey certain *gessa*, which were either prohibitions or positive actions to be carried out. Cuchulainn's *gess* was never to look on a naked woman. This did not prevent him from fully enjoying sexual relationships, of course, which had to be confined to the darkness. We hear that when he returned from his first foray as a warrior, he was seen from afar coming in his chariot and was under the influence of battle-madness. To prevent him running amok in the royal seat, his king, Conor Mac Nessa, ordered all the women to go out to meet him naked. Cuchulainn masked his eyes against this rather unusual display and when thus engaged, he was seized by the men of Ulster and dumped in a cauldron of cold water to cool his crazy ardour.[8] One wonders whether this story preserves the memory of a general taboo among certain ancient peoples in Ireland against gazing on a woman's nudity.

As will be discussed later on, the advent of Christianity brought about an attempt to change many of the attitudes of the Gaelic people concerning sex and marriage. For the present it is interesting to recall the fact that the native Gaelic word for 'kiss' *[memm]* has not been used for centuries. One does not wish to draw too many conclusions from this, of course, but it is a notable fact that the word used is a borrowing from ecclesiastical Latin. *Póg* (originally *póc*) is derived from *pac* (a Latin borrowing filtered through the Welsh language), the stem of *pacis* which in its turn comes from the liturgical term *osculum pacis* – 'the kiss of peace', a ceremonial kiss exchanged during the Mass and far removed from the healthy and sexual labial encounters which take place between men and women. The writer of the first comparative dictionary in Europe, Cormac Mac Cullenan, king-bishop of Cashel in the end of the ninth century, chastely points out that the word *póc* is eminently suitable because, he says, a kiss is a sign of peace![9]

It should be stressed that there is a complete range of terms for all sexual matters. The clerics did not succeed in replacing these with coy words borrowed from the language of their liturgy. At this point it should also be noted that dancing also lacks a native term and no one is likely to assert that dancing, no less than kissing, was unknown to the primitive Irish. It sets one thinking how significant it must be that the frequent preliminaries to love-making, especially in primitive society, dancing and kissing, are known to Gaelic speakers for over a thousand years by words other than native ones.

CRIMES AND MISDEMEANOURS

Crimes and misdemeanours against a person's sexual well-being and rights are treated in the brehon laws. We can get a glimpse of the type of society for which these laws were framed by noting some of the matters mentioned throughout the various tracts.

While there is no mention anywhere of barbaric crimes, such as the excision of the clitoris or the removal of female breasts, there is a rather interesting article on the penalties for castration. Each possible eventuality is foreseen in the tract:

i) If a man's penis is cut off, the wretched sufferer is entitled to two kinds of compensation for his loss. Naturally, his full honour-price had to be paid and in addition to this the atonement called *corp-díre* in full. The term used for 'penis' in this tract is *uidim* and it should be noted that it is a word which could also mean 'implement, instrument or tool.'

ii) The case of him whose scrotum is cut off comes next. For some odd reason only full *corp-díre* is payable in this case. One wonders how the victim's honour is unaffected in such a situation. Perhaps this was rare and even unknown. In many places in the brehon law tracts the legislators set out examples which are merely notional and dredged up from their inventive lawyers' minds.

iii) The tract then discusses the fellow whose left testicle only is removed. For this deed the penalty was full body-price or *corp-díre*. The reason for this has its roots in medical theory. It was thought that the left testicle was the active agent in procreation and they evidently regarded the companion as a balancing ornament.

iv) As might be anticipated the removal of the right testicle earned a penalty which was equal to part of the body-price. A man's fertility, the lawyers reasoned, was not seriously affected by this act.

v) The final detail is that a much diminished penalty for full castration is payable to a man in Holy Orders or a decrepit old fellow. Reasonably enough it is stated that such a person had no need of his generative organs. For the removal of his excess organs the castrator was penalised according the severity of the wound inflicted on his victim, as he would be in the case of wounding any other part of the body.[10]

The brehon laws distinguished between two types of rape. One was the violent possession of a woman sexually and the other was to make love to her by deceit when she was asleep and could not give her consent.

In the old stories, which may be historical or at least based on what happened in the earliest times, there is a story of rape which is worth retelling. We hear that Ailill Olum – Bare-eared Ailill – earned his sobriquet in the following manner. Ailill defeated and slew a rival king in battle. He then laid hands on the dead man's daughter and proceeded to rape her. This spirited young lady resisted him so violently that she bit off his two ears and earned him his unusual nickname. Ailill was so infuriated by her assault on his person that he transfixed her with his spear to the ground and killed her instantly. The point of his spear struck a stone underneath her and was bent. He attempted to straighten the spear-point with his teeth but this blackened his teeth and his breath became foul henceforth. It is tempting to see all this as an allegory. The old story relates that Ailill was bound by *gessa* or taboos not to bend his spear; not to straighten his spear-point with his teeth. All these he had violated.[11] It is difficult not to see the spear as a phallic symbol, the stone as an unwilling woman, and his slaying of her as his attempted rape. What the significance of the fouling of his breath and the black-ening of his teeth may be, can be left to the vaulting imag-ination of the individual reader.

We should consider for a moment the practical appli-cation of an honour-price on a rapist. First of all, the fine could be a burden on the rapist and his kindred, because they all participated in helping to pay it. The individual before the law did not have the same significance then as it does now. The girl's kindred and family saw to it that justice was done. The rapist was notified of the charge against him and of the penalty to be exacted. If he did not pay after a number of days, the plaintiff could come and fast at his doorstep, to use a modern expression. If he still remained obdurate, the value of the penalty could be seized in valuables or driven off as cattle. This, of course, could lead to trouble and bloodshed. There was no quest-ion of imprisonment or corporal punishment of any kind. Social pressures were expected to force the rapist to face the penalty when it became due. This applied, of course, to all crimes and misdemeanours. The technically legal fairness and occasional practical unfairness of our modern law were avoided. One could not, for example, 'fix' a case. Likewise, there was no judge or jury who had to apply the same penalties to rich and poor alike, often to the grave disadvantage of the latter. Finally, there was no inane system like the modern prison. The working of the ancient Irish laws was described by English jurists in the early seventeenth century as 'compounding the felony' and they hastened to apply their own legal practice, which they re-garded as the best, considering the remnants of the brehon laws as something barbarous.

There is one example of sexual misdemeanour ment-ioned which is worth notice. We are told that if a man shaves off the pubic hair of a woman in order to seduce her, he incurred full honour-price and body-price for his barbering stint and his resultant fun.[12] This may have its origin in some primitive prohibition contrary to that found in the Islamic religion. To anyone who comes on this little matter in the ancient laws, it seems strange and somewhat hilarious. The penalty seems out of all proportion to the deed; it is equal to that imposed on him who castrates a man fully. More understandable to our minds is the prohibition on anyone putting his hand under a woman's clothes to seduce her. The term used for seduction in this case is *meblaige,* which means also 'shaming' or the like.[13]

As in many primitive societies and in our own times incest was regarded with horror by the ancient Irish. There are many anecdotes from olden times which illustrate the attitude of the people to this matter. Again it must be stressed that one is not necessarily accepting these as history but they reflect the mores of ancient Ireland.

It is said that Conor Mac Nessa had twenty-one sons in all. Not satisfied with the services of his numerous paramours and wives, it is said that he slept with his mother one time when he was drunk. The storytellers inform us that for this act he was punished by the fact that only three of his sons survived into manhood.[14] Another king, Aengus Tuirbech, took his own daughter as a bed-companion and the result was the birth of a son. We are told that the infant was put in a boat on the sea with valuables suitable to a king about him. It is said that fishermen rescued him and reared the boy as their own.[15]

A story about the origin of Lughaidh Riabh nDerg tells us that he was conceived in incest. The combined efforts of his mother's three brothers when they were drunk, made her pregnant. The child bore on him for life a red circle on the skin around his neck and another about his waist.[16]

There is a story recorded of a Munster king of ancient times which may enshrine a pre-Christian custom among some of the ancient peoples whenever incest occurred. Caibre Musc was King of Munster, it is said, and he slept with his sister. As a result she bore him twin sons. One of the little ones was burned alive and its ashes thrown into a river. The other child was hidden by a druid and spirited away to an island where a woman cared for it. After a year it was taken to its grandmother who took it in care from that time onwards.[17]

Of the stories mentioned above only one mentions a custom of actually killing the child of an incestuous union. The circumstances of each case may be termed that of rape and inebriation is often given as the cause of the deed. One doesn't wish to draw unwarranted conclusions from so few cases, but it is interesting to note that there is nowhere any case of incest coming out of a genuine love between a couple. It is impossible to know what customs regulated the course of events to be followed in very early times regarding the child of incest. The Munster story may give us quite a useful hint as to what it was.

One is struck by the absence of reference throughout the ancient texts to homosexuality, if one makes an exception of ecclesiastical documents. What is one to understand from this? It is hardly possible that it was unknown! Masturbation provides a very good example of the basic change in attitudes which has come upon the Irish people over the centuries and which is reflected in the Gaelic language. In the dictionary of modern Gaelic compiled by Professor Tomás de Bhaldraithe, the word for masturbation is *féin-truailliú* – literally, 'self-pollution'. In ancient times it was known as *lám-chairdes,* which means literally, 'manual sex' or 'manual love', a much more tolerant and gentle term than the vicious and condemnatory modern word.

This section can be suitably concluded by quoting two quatrains of verse from the period in Irish life under review. They seem to sum up contrary attitudes – one of the natural human being and the other of Christian Church. The amorous Etaín of the storytellers is thus spoken of:

> I don't know
> Who will sleep with Etaín Bán;
> But I know that Etaín Bán
> Will not be sleeping on her own.

Next we read the words of a monk who is awakened on a windy winter's night to go to the oratory for prayers. At that hour other men were also arising to visit their loved ones:

> A sweet little bell
> Is rung on a windy night;
> I prefer to tryst with it
> Than tryst with a foolish lady.

WOMAN BEFORE THE LAW

There is a very interesting list of women who have forfeited their right to the legal compensations of *corp-díre* and honour-price in the brehon laws. Since it is women who often get the worst part of situations in marital and purely sexual partnerships in our type of society, it is worth looking at the article in full.[18]

In line with the passion for mystical numbers of the writers of the ancient laws, seven types of women are listed. (1) One is she who steals. For a first offence the lady loses one-third of her legal rights and all of them after a third offence. (2) The biting satirising type is next mentioned; she is described as one 'who carves every shape'! ('Carves' is a picturesque term to evoke the viciousness of the satirist.) (3) The third type is a treacherous woman. (4) The fourth is the false tale-bearer whose people must pay for her malicious gossip. (5) We next come to the fifth type who is succinctly described as a 'bush-strumpet'. This lady is one who has sex with anyone who is available in the seclusion of the natural cover of the countryside. By the way, a harlot, prostitute or strumpet received little mercy from the brehon laws. Two definitions of such a person are found. In one she is described as a 'known unchaste woman'. This is expanded in another place with great tolerance to the statement that a harlot is one who has intercourse with three or four men in the course of one day or night! (6) The sixth type of woman who loses her legal rights is she who wounds and (7) the last one is she who is so mean that she refuses food to every person who asks for it.

The foregoing list is rather illuminating. It illustrates the type of society of which we speak and seems like delineating implicitly a set of seven commandments for Irish women in early times:

1. Do not steal.
2. Do not satirise or abuse unjustly.
3. Do not betray your own people.
4. Do not spread false and malicious gossip.
5. Do not sleep with every fellow who wishes you to do so.
6. Do not draw a knife on anyone.
7 Do not refuse food to those who ask and need your hospitality.

We could add that these equally apply to men!

MARRIAGE

IT IS HARDLY NECESSARY to state that wooing has no place in
the early Irish law-tracts and we must look to the storytellers of these times to fill this gap in our knowledge.
Stories of wooing were considered so important by the
professional storytellers that a separate section of every
raconteur's repertory consisted of tales of wooing. It should
be stated here that these gentlemen were not just naturally
gifted yarners and tale-spinners but a separate class of the
aos dána, 'the artistic class', as poets, historians, musicians
and storytellers were collectively described. The story sum-
marised below, *The Wooing of Emer*, was written in the
eleventh century manuscript called *The Book of the Dun
Cow*, but the language and atmosphere of the tale suggest
that much of it is very ancient indeed. It may thus be taken
as a tale mirroring life in the period under discussion in
this work[1]

The Wooing of Emer describes how the hero, Cuchulainn, found himself a wife. We are first of all introduced to
a council of the principal men of Ulster, who have met to
consider how Cuchulainn might be suitably married. They
give their reasons why he should take a partner. First of
all, marriage would safeguard their own wives and daughters from his attentions because he was much fancied by
the women of Ulster. Secondly, they considered the importance of the hero fathering a son to inherit his father's
prowess as a warrior. In this part of the tale we probably
have an echo of a custom of arranging the marriage of a
young man before he showed signs of sexual maturity, because it is clear that Cuchulainn, although attractive to the
ladies at this stage, was not yet ripe for marriage.

Cuchulainn's good qualities, which caused him to be

admired by the women, are then enumerated. He had wisdom, good sense, a good appearance, and was skilled in chess-playing and juggling. He also had great strength, ability to estimate an enemy's strength correctly, and the gift of prophecy. Cuchulainn's faults were three in number: he was too daring, too beautiful and his testicles were not yet fully developed! It is said that strangers mocked him over the latter deficiency. This leads one to surmise that marriages may have been arranged before reaching sexual maturity.

We are then told that nine eligible girls were introduced to Cuchulainn from each province but that he showed no interest in any of them. He then went to seek a lady for himself and visited Emer who had the qualities he most admired: a good figure, a pleasing voice, the ability to sing sweetly, skill at embroidery, wisdom and virginity. Doubtlessly these qualities were sought by prospective husbands in the days when this story was told.

Cuchulainn arrived with noisy demonstrations at Emer's house in his chariot-neighing horses, rattling of chariot, grinding of the wheels and so on. We are told that a blaze of love lighted up his face. When Emer became aware of Cuchulainn's intentions, she pointed out that she was a younger daughter whose sister should be preferred to her, doubtlessly also a reflection of ancient custom of precedence. She then conducts a dignified dialogue with Cuchulainn, during which they exchange details of their backgrounds. Emer speaks of her high rank and the status of her fosterage, all equal to that of a queen. She impressed Cuchulainn so much by her spritely conversation that he suggested bluntly: 'Why don't we have intercourse together? Up till now I have not met a girl who could hold her own in a conversation with me!' The humour of this is apparent. One can notice his overdaring; after all he was incapable of making love to a woman properly at this stage! Emer retorted to the suggestion with a question as to whether he had a wife. When she heard that he had not, she then took refuge in the excuse that her sister was older than she. She was informed that Cuchulainn loved her and not her sister.

After this Cuchulainn went abroad and learned more of the warrior-profession and also had a love-affair with a fairy-like lady by whom he had a son. Mature at last he returned to Ireland for his bride. He journeyed with her to Emain Macha, the seat of the King of Ulster, Conor Mac Nessa. Here, while he was looking forward to his first night with his bride, he was reminded that each bride in Ulster must spend her first night with the king. In fact, Conor Mac Nessa was under *gess* – taboo – to exercise the *droit de seigneur*, that is the right of the lord to sleep with the bride on her first night. When he heard this, Cuchulainn leaped from the couch were he was resting and sent the feathers in it flying throughout the room. The furious hero left the house in agitation. Conor Mac Nessa then asked him to collect game for him from afar. When he was gone, a druid attempted to save the king from violating his *gess* while satisfying Cuchulainn's outraged feelings. The compromise reached was that the king should indeed occupy the same bed with Emer that night but the druid should also sleep there to restrain the king from sexual activity. This succeeded and on the next morning Conor paid Emer the bride-price known as *tinnscra*, which should have been paid by her husband and was due, apparently, to all brides from 'outside', i.e., from another *tuath*. He also paid Cuchulainn an honour-price. The couple slept together that night and the storyteller informs us: 'They never separated again until death'. This appears to be the only source in the ancient literature where the *droit de signeur* is mentioned. It may have been widespread in prehistoric Ireland, in the period before any records were kept.

A much more striking and better known story of wooing is that of Deirdre, the *femme fatale* of the Ulstermen.[2] It contains details and an atmosphere which are worth relating. It was predicted at her birth that she would bring death and destruction on the Ulstermen. King Conor Mac Nessa was present and he decided to cheat the prophecy by putting her into seclusion and then marrying her himself when she was mature! In her solitary existence with only a foster-father and mother for companions her thoughts turned to a man as she began to grow up. She described what her ideal man should be like: skin as white as snow, hair as black as raven's feathers, face as ruddy as blood. In alarm her foster-mother, to whom she said this, informed her that she had described exactly one of the Ulster warriors, Neesha *(Noíse)*. Deirdre expressed the desire to have Neesha for herself. Eventually her opportunity came. One day Neesha came wandering through the wood where she lived and Deirdre saw him. She pretended to ignore him as he passed by. The following earthy conversation then took place:

'That's a nice summer-heifer that's passing by us!' said he.

'The big summer-heifers,' she answered, 'belong where the bull is.'

'You have the bull of the province!' said he, meaning Conor Mac Nessa.

'I'd choose a young bull like you, if I had a choice between you!' she cried.

'No!' said he. 'What about the druid's prophecy?'

'Are you saying that to reject me?' said she.

'Let it be that way then!' he said.

At this she leaped at him and grasped his head by the two ears.

'If you don't bring me with you,' she exclaimed, 'these two ears are shame and derision to you!'

'Get away from me, woman!' he cried.

'I'll have you in that case!' she said.

This is the seduction of a man by one, who, as W. B.

Yeats said, was 'proud and stiff/When on love intent'. It is based on the normal language between aristocrats in the ninth century, because this tale, like all the Ulster tales, was written for aristocrats and about aristocrats. This was no peasant literature, although it is bucolic in the extreme. Nowadays this type of imagery is well-known in Ireland but confined to the countryside, of course, and used among people who are not exactly the same as the ruling classes in Ireland in the early times.

THE MARRIAGE CONTRACT

The brehon laws determine exactly those who may contract a proper marriage and under what conditions. The word for 'marriage' is *lánamnus* and can be translated fairly accurately but awkwardly as a social connection for the purposes of procreation.

Since it is the man who may take the initiative in love-making, certain disabilities are detailed which prohibited a man from making a valid marriage, or invalidated any marital contract made in spite of any one of these. The lawyers distinguished seven different cases:

i) A barren man. This applied to someone contracting another marriage when it had already been apparent that he could not procreate. It could also give an excuse for annulling a marriage after it was clear that it was barren and would be likely to remain so.

ii) An unarmed man. This euphemism covered the case of one who was impotent.

iii) A man in Holy Orders. This case is due to the influence of the Christian Church when the law of celibacy became strictly enforced after the fifth century, perhaps. It should be noted that the laws, as we have them today, were written down in times when the country was largely Christianised. This should never be forgotten.

iv) A churchman. This means a bishop. This could be included in the previous entry but the lawyers loved mystical numbers like seven and by adding this extra item they achieved their objective.

v) A rockman. This picturesque term is given to someone who has no land. The laws applied generally only to what were called the *Féni*, i.e., all freemen, whether of noble or plebian status. Consequently no man worth anything would be without his share of land in one form of tenure or another.

vi) A very fat man. The laws explain that such a man is disqualified because he is too obese to perform the sexual act.

vii) *A claenán*. This word means 'perverted little wretch' and this severe term describes the man who discloses his woman's bed-secrets. This fellow forfeited the right to marriage or invalidated any contract made by his indiscreet blabbing.[3]

In the laws it is abundantly clear that the mark of a man of standing was that he had a *cétmuinter* according to the laws. This word means a spouse who is his chief wife and, presumably, the first one he marries. A glance at the laws will make this point clear. The highest of the noble grades was the *aire forggaill* and among his principal attributes is having a 'chief spouse according to the law'.[4] After him in rank came the *aire túise*, concerning whom a similar statement is made.[5] The *aire désa* was the lowest of the noble ranks and he is also ideally one who has a legally contracted chief spouse.[6] The chief commoner or plebian among the freemen was the *bóaire*. He is distinguished by having a chief spouse in accordance with the law and it is also specified that she should be of equal rank with himself.

The contracts must have involved much hard bargaining especially in the case of a *cétmuinter*. Geoffrey Keating in his history of Ireland, *Foras Feasa ar Éirinn*, concerning the great Fair of Tailten says that the young boys and girls of marriageable age were kept apart until the contracts were made. The site of this fair is traditionally around Teltown in County Meath and an early source speaks of a hillock in the area called 'Hillock of the Bride-Price' where the dowries were paid.[7] An old tradition in the Teltown area also preserved the memory of where the marriages were performed and the name 'Marriage Hollow' was given to it.[8]

It has already been mentioned in the story of the *Wooing of Emer* that Emer told Cuchulainn that she had an elder sister who should be married before herself. This probably enshrines a custom that the elder girl married first and the others according to age afterwards. In the old story of the origin of the Boru tribute it is stated that the King of Leinster sought a wife from the King of Meath and had to marry the elder, although the younger of his two daughters was the more beautiful. The King of Leinster then faked the death of his wife and arranged a marriage with the second one. When he acquired her and brought her home, she met her sister by accident. Both were so smitten with shame that they died at once.[9] This led to the imposition of a heavy tribute, which led to warfare between Meath and Leinster for centuries afterwards.

The Cashel lexicographer of the ninth century – Cormac Mac Cullenan – informs us that the favourite time for weddings was in November.[10] This would make sense in a pastoral civilisation. The summer and autumn work was completed, the cows and their attendants had returned from summer-pastures, and the wealth of the people was at its optimum.

It already has been noted that the honour-price of a spouse was half that of her man but his applies only to a *cétmuinter*. The law tract from which the foregoing details have been noted also lets us see that other types of male-female partnerships were recognised as well. We are informed that a *dormuine* or concubine was entitled to one-quarter of her partner's honour-price.[11] When it is remembered that the brehon laws were finally codified in Christian times, it seems amazing that the traditions of the Irish people were so strong as to run contrary to Christian marriage law in matters such as this.

The general notion behind the brehon law enactment's regarding sexual relations between men and women was not to close the mind to the fact that certain variations occurred in the affections of men and women towards one another, but to recognise them and legislate for them instead of simply condemning them as illegal. Ten different cases of *lánamnus* or marriage or sexual partnerships were cited as subject to legislation:[12]

i) A union of equal rank. In this case the couple were equal in rank and property and this type of union or marriage was encouraged and was the ideal.

ii) A woman supported on a man's property. Needless to remark, this union was between partners of different classes in society.

iii) A man supported on a woman's property. This is the reverse of the preceding but in this case it is stipulated that the man must do the work on the woman's property, such as tilling the land and tending the cattle. He was not just a 'kept-man'.

iv) A woman received in place of a wife. This was the concubine and her status was recognised and her rights as a person safeguarded. She had several titles: *dormuine* has already been mentioned. A much more gentle and true title was *ben charrthach* – the loved woman, a term synonymous with *die Geliebte* in German. English and Irish Law have the term 'common law wife', it is true, but she has no more rights than that of any other woman in the eyes of the legislators. The brehon lawyers were far more realistic and far more conscious of the rights of a woman in this position than our modern legislators.

v) The man who kept company with another woman but who does not live with her permanently and neither of them is wholly supported by the other. This kind of union is accepted by the modern legislators and decried by the moralists of our time, who either ignore it or condemn it.

vi) The abducted woman. She also has legal rights and neither she nor her offspring are ignored nor slurred by the brehon laws.

vii) The wandering soldier and his woman. Evidently this type of union had to be specifically recognised because all the other partnerships were between people who had a stake in the rural community. The soldier and his wife were footloose people who did not fit into the normal type of community in ancient Ireland.

viii) Union of deception. The title implies that a man began the sexual partnership by some ruse such as having intercourse with a woman who was asleep. He incurred specific obligations to her and her child or children in this case.

ix) Forced union. This, of course, means rape. While the perpetrator was punished for the violence offered and the breach of honour to the girl and her kindred, any child or children born of the illicit union is recognised and the situation regularised.

x) The union of levity. This is explained as a sexual partnership between idiots or lunatics.

The principal comment to be made on the ten cases quoted above is that there could be no such thing as an 'illegitimate child'. All children born to a woman, no matter what the circumstances of their conception, were legislated for and their rights recognised. The lawgivers were not hamstrung by the idea of a single lawful marriage, the issue of which were alone 'legitimate'. All children were 'legitimate'. Victorian and modern English and Irish laws made maintenance orders against the putative fathers of children born out of wedlock, and that was all. The child was not recognised in his birth-certificate as the offspring of his father. The column for that detail was left blank, as if the mother had conceived through parthenogenesis! Such a crazy situation did not exist in ancient Ireland. It is interesting to note how often the English State Papers in the sixteenth century speak of men as the 'base sons' of some chief. In effect, these sons were not base according to brehon law in the areas of Ireland where the old laws were still in operation. In late years, at long last, the stigma of illegitimacy has been removed from children born outside marriage. No longer is the space on the birth certificate for the father's name left blank. The child is no longer abused, at least tacitly, by a society where men once had the upper hand. Unmarried partners living together as permanently committed couples are also recognised by the southern state.

In all the unions listed above a contract was made between the two people, at least retrospectively. At this stage the general customs regarding the contracting of the marriage of a *cétmuinter* must be examined. The business aspects apply in different degrees in all the other unions.

i) *Coibche:* this was the word for the principal dowry of a bride. It is glossed with the word 'buy' in the ninth century. The prospective husband paid a *coibche* to the girl's father, who then divided it with the *áige fine* ('head of kindred' or sometimes translated inaccurately, 'head of the tribe'). The interesting thing about the *coibche* was that it continued to be paid each year for twenty-one years in all, if the marriage lasted that length of time. In the second year the wife kept a third of the amount for herself, while her father and his superior divided the remainder. As years went by, the wife kept a larger part of each year's *coibche*.[13] She thus kept adding to her personal property out of her husband's reserves. One wonders what significance the twenty-one year term had. Perhaps the lawyers felt that past this term the marriage was really durable beyond a doubt. In this period also the wife's chief vigour as housewife and mother were brought into play. At the end of twenty-one years she had amassed a considerable amount of property and could be quite independent if her husband decided to give his attentions to a younger woman. It should be noted that giving a *coibche* for a woman was tantamount to contracting a sexual partnership with her. The historian, Geoffrey Keating, mentions that when a king in ancient Ireland wished to sleep with a woman he had her *ar choibche*, i.e., *coibche* – contracted, as it were.

ii) *Tinól:* this dowry was a kind of wedding-present to the bride and was presented by her friends and acquaintances. It consisted of cattle, the chief wealth of the time. It was divided between the bride and her father, one-third going to the father and the bride taking the rest.[14]

iii) *Tinchor:* this wedding-portion of the bride consisted, apparently, of household goods. It was confused in later times with *tinól.* It should be noted that the technical term in the brehon laws for a woman supported on a man's property was *ben for fertinchur* and the other case was *fer for bentinchur.* In these contexts the word *tinchor* seems to mean simply means of livelihood and support.[15]

iv) *Tinnscra:* this kind of dowry or bride-payment has already been briefly mentioned in the story of the *Wooing of Emer.* It was made to the father of the bride when she was from outside the *tuath.* We hear that it consisted of articles of gold, silver, copper and brass.[16] Later historians stated that the first *tinnscra* paid in Ireland was given to the women that Gaelic invaders found before them to induce them to marry them voluntarily. It is significant that the payment consisted of easily transportable wealth, unlike cows and household goods.

DUTIES OF HUSBAND AND WIFE
The principal obligations of the married couple or cohabiting partners are specified in the brehon laws. The woman gives her man *toil ocus genus ocus bangním. Toil*

35

means desire – sexual desire; *genus* means chastity – she must reserve her sexual experience for him alone while the contract lasts; *bangním* – literally 'woman-deed', i.e., sexual relations. Where her man is concerned only *fergním* is specified – the virile act.[17] However it is also pointed out that, although she must accept his primacy and leadership because of his manhood, she can still take an oath against him. She does not lose this basic right because it is noted that their marital partnership is only a contract and does not deprive her of any rights she might have possessed if she had been other than his wife.[18]

With regard specifically to partners of equal status, it is decreed that all contracts made by either must be made with the knowledge of both parties. Any concealment nullifies a contract.[19] One very important contract made by both was that regarding the fostering of their children and this had to be settled jointly. The mother had a direct voice in any arrangements made in this matter.

Naturally the brehon laws favoured a marriage between equal partners. It simplified all matters between both considerably. In an equal partnership the wife is described as *comthigerna* – co-lord. Both must provide jointly food for the great festivals, collaborate equally in the buying of breeding cattle, the collection of household effects and pig-litters to fatten. Any ox or horse, which was useless for ploughing, might not be sold without consultation and then the price must be used for the benefit of both. Where tillage was concerned, the couple must agree on what form the co-operation with others in the work should be. If they sought co-operation outside their kindred, it must be allowed by the wife only if the husband receives favourable terms.[20] All the minutiae of the life of a couple depending on the land for their livelihood were cared for meticulously by the brehon laws so as to protect the rights of the wife against any exploitation of her by her husband or his kindred.

The safe-delivery of the unborn child was of great consideration to the society regulated by the brehon laws. Needless to say there is nothing whatever mentioned about contraception nor what has been termed 'procured abortion' in the modern sense. It is otherwise with abortion in a general manner.

The tract which mentions the aborting of the unborn foetus seems to refer more to what is sometimes described as 'miscarriage' than anything else. The laws are clear on this subject: no woman or man had any right to terminate a pregnancy or to cause it to terminate. Notice the following cases cited in the brehon laws:[21]

i) If a woman refuses food so as to abort the foetus, both honour and body-prices must be paid by her to the father's kindred, a *cumal* to her own kindred, and her husband received his own honour-price and the equivalent of a *coibche*. These heavy penalties reflect the attitude of the people to abortion. We are informed also that if a woman refuses food but not with the intention of causing her to abort the foetus, the penalties for miscarriage of the child are as follows: half the fines for the two kindreds and a *coibche* for her husband. The next case cited is that of the woman who refuses food because she is too timid or shy to seek it! In this case, if the foetus is aborted, the father's kindred receives a *cumal*, the mother's a seventh of a *cumal* and the husband a *coibche*.

ii) The case of the husband who may be culpable of an abortion or miscarriage is then considered. When he refuses his wife food in order to cause an abortion, the penalties are similar to that of the first case in the previous article, except that the wife receives a *coibche* and also her own honour-price. If he refuses her food, the penalties resemble the third case in the previous articles, except that he must compensate his wife with a *coibche*.

It is specifically stated that the above cases apply only

in the cases of recognised sexual partnerships mentioned in the beginning of this chapter. So broad are these that there is one kind of partnership that seems to be outside their scope – that of the man and his prostitute. The prostitute was looked on with disfavour, not because of her active sex-life, but because of her varied sex-life. Any relationship that was exclusive for its duration was recognised. The prostitute did not qualify for recognition, therefore. In reading the provisions of the brehon laws regarding abortion, one is bemused by the rather odd details. As in other cases, one often asks how far the lawyer was citing cases which had occurred or were likely to occur, and how often he was concocting examples from his own tortuous lawyer's mind. In another place the much more practical reason for an abortion is mentioned – physical violence intentionally inflicted to cause this result or physical violence having this result but not this intention. The case of the couple engaging in some violent game with malice aforethought or otherwise, is also cited and provided for.[22]

The brehon laws have some very humane provisions about a woman in labour. For example, a man who was seeking women for midwife duties could not be legally distrained for some debt.[23] This was also extended to the whole period during which his wife was in labour.[24]

Regarding the circumstances surrounding the birth, we cannot depend on the brehon laws for information but must turn to the old literature. One of the oldest is the description of the scenes in the house where Deirdre was born.[25] We are told that the mother was entertaining Conor Mac Nessa and his nobles before she was born. As housewife, it was her duty to direct the activities of her servants and this she was doing although she was in advanced pregnancy. As the old writer graphically describes the scenes of wild revelry: 'Goblets and platters were being circulated and shouts of drunkenness were raised'. Then suddenly labour pains set in and she rushed through the hall to go to her bed. As she did so, the child screamed in her womb. This brought the drunken revellers to their senses and they forced her to wait until the druid foretold the future of her unborn child. He placed his hand on the mother's stomach and foretold that a girl would be born. He then added that she would be the cause of great slaughter to the men of Ulster. The feasting warriors demanded that the child should be put to death immediately after birth. Conor rejected this demand and announced instead that he would have her fostered until she was old enough to co-habit with him.

Another barbaric story is told about the birth of a Munster king. This was Fiachaidh Muillethan (F. the broad-crowned). His father had fallen in battle before his birth and his mother found herself on the banks of the River Suir near Knockgraffon (south of Athassell) when her time had come. A druid foretold that she would have a son and that he would be king later if his mother delayed his birth for twenty-four hours The poor girl took him seriously and went into the river where she sat on a boulder to prevent the birth taking place too soon. When the child was born, his head was flat-topped and remained so for the remainder of his life. As for his mother, she died soon after her brutal ordeal but her son became king.[26]

There is another legendary tale which tells us that a mother struck her new-born child's head with a boulder to bring good luck on him in life! It is said that he became a king afterwards but that he always bore a hollow in the part of his head where the rock touched him. No hair grew on this area, we are assured.[27]

Having mentioned these rather lurid accounts of the births of some of Ireland's legendary folk, one is left with a complete blank about the usual circumstances of the birth of children. The medical treatises extant from olden times date from the thirteenth and fourteenth centuries and are translations or adaptations of texts known and used in England and France.

Reference has already been made to the *cess noínden*. Whether this is a single reference to the practice of the couvade among the pre-Christian Irish or not, one has no way of knowing now. All that can be asserted on this subject is that, if the couvade was practised, it disappeared without trace unlike a very large number of other pre-Christian practices of early times.

FOSTERAGE

The parents of those who followed the brehon laws never reared their own children, but had them fostered. This was the custom in parts of Ireland up to the sixteenth century. The custom of fosterage was condemned by the English authorities in Ireland and viewed with the greatest disfavour. The bond between foster-child and foster-parents is said to have been stronger than that between him or her and the natural ones.

The choice of fosterers, as has been noted already, had to be a joint decision of husband and wife or of the parents of the child. Here it is worth noting that in some unions, such as that which originated in forcible abduction or rape, the parents might not prolong their union legally into a 'normal' marriage. In this case the child's upbringing was not affected because it was reared by foster-parents whatever its origin.

The foster-children stayed with their guardians until they were seventeen years of age.[28] The fee was generally twelve cows, seventeen 'screphalls' (screphall = one twenty-fourth of an ounce of silver or milch cow), and a working horse. To have the child properly provided for, a little coverlet was sent with it, a milch cow specifically to supply milk for it when it was weaned, and a cooking vessel. After weaning the child received three times the full of the vessel each day in gruel. When he grew older this amount was baked for him. The vessel must be thirty-two centimetres in diameter and big enough to hold the milk yield of the cow for a day.[29] (It should be stated that milk yields in these times were presumably much lower than nowadays.) Where the fosterage of a young girl was concerned the charges made were heavier because she had to have more attention.[30]

Apart from questions of rank in society, the foster-son had a status which varied with his age. The brehon laws saw three separate ages of development. Up to the age of seven the boy was punished corporally for his misdemeanours. He had to receive three warnings first and when he did not heed these, he was beaten. Between the ages of seven and twelve the boy was not allowed to be given corporal punishment for what he did amiss. Instead of this he was deprived of food. Anyone who knows the appetites of small boys between these ages understands how effective this punishment was then. In the final age between twelve and seventeen the boy had to pay compensation according to the law like an adult. He thus left fosterage trained to carry himself as a responsible adult. His upbringing, as laid down in the brehon laws, was neither permissive nor severe. Much could be learned from it by modern educational theorists who are reacting unwisely from the old harsh measures of the recent past. The misdemeanours mentioned as likely to be committed by a foster-child are theft and assault.[31]

It was also provided for in the brehon laws that exemption from corporal punishment be granted to the sons of kings.[32] By implication this was also extended to girls. The sons of others must be punished in such a manner that no marks are left on them. Compensation for marking and also for nicknaming them was decreed.[33] The latter provision seems to have been made to guard against having a child vilified by a sobriquet.

It is of some interest to note that the Gaelic term for foster-father was *aite*. This word, written as *oide* nowadays, means simply 'teacher', a word which expresses all that a good teacher should be. While speaking of words, the Gaelic word in modern times for 'marriage' should be noted: *pósadh*. This is derived from *sponsa* and dates from the coming of the Norman invasion. *Sponsa* was the wife who was married for life and for whom there was no divorce. This reflects the narrow view of man-woman relationships which culminated in such hateful concepts as the 'unmarried mother' and 'illegitimate child'. The ancient Irish were far too humane and realistic to tolerate such ideas.

There were certain women who had to make their own provisions for the fosterage of their children without the help or collaboration of their men. Most of the cases cited are self-evident while the others throw some light on the attitudes of the people of early Ireland.

As usual we find the types of women in this case neatly made out in seven:[34]

i) The freewoman who bears a child for a slave without the knowledge of his master must have her child fostered without reference to the father who cannot help anyway. Evidently the master who knows and condones the affair must provide assistance; hence the insistence on his knowledge to save the woman from embarrassment.

ii) A child born of a man who has been forbidden to cohabit with the woman by his father must be provided for by the mother alone. It is clear that in this case the woman also must be aware that the man has been forbidden to have any dealings with her.

iii) The son of a harlot is also considered her own and no one's responsibility but hers. The clear impossibility of deciding paternity is the obvious reason here.

iv) The son of a *cú glas:* a *cú glas* was the picturesque term used for a foreigner. It means literally 'grey hound'. He was a casual visitor and could and did leave the country when his ship sailed or his business was done. The mother of his child was all on her own and could not claim anything to pay for the fosterage of the child. She must provide for this herself.

v) The son of a *rindile*: For some reason the son of a satirist who observes neither justice nor fair play but sacrifices everyone without mercy must be fostered by his mother without the collaboration of his father.

vi) The son of a man who is an outcast from his people. Obviously this man has lost what we call nowadays his 'civil rights' and is incapable of making a legal contract of any kind. The mother is not left to bear the burden alone, however, if she is ignorant at the time of conception that her lover is an outcast.

vii) The son of a man in Holy Orders, who has slept with a girl when he had that status and has not returned to the lay state but is doing penance for his deed. The mother must also bear the burden in this case alone.

In these cases it seems the principal consideration is the possibility of having the man within the jurisdiction. The man in Holy Orders was technically in another jurisdiction, that of the church or monastery, and he was disqualified from forming any sexual relationship with a woman anyway.

Cuckoldry, Adultery and Abduction

In Irish society not so long ago a husband could sue a man for 'criminal conversation' with his wife, that is seducing or enticing her from him, because she was considered his chattel property. This law, which protected the ownership of a wife by her husband, was still in force in Ireland when it had been repealed in England. The brehon laws took a far more realistic view of the whole business and acted accordingly.

In a few words, the child born to a woman of another man besides her husband, was considered her husband's child until it was claimed and proved to be someone else's. Then the real father must buy the child from him.[1]

From the context it appears that the child is already some time in fosterage when the matter is cleared up. The price paid for the child was equal to the honour-and body-prices of the man that was cuckolded. To this was added the amount already expended on the fosterage of the child. It was also decreed that the real father should receive back all he had paid because of his adultery with another man's woman.

The law quoted above was applicable to a cuckold who is of the noble and commoner grades in society, a foreigner, a person outside the *tuath*, or a person of the *dóer* class. It should be explained that a person of the latter class was not a slave, as the word seems to imply, but someone who held property, such as cattle, for which he paid his patron a yearly fee.

One problem could arise in the case of buying back a son born of cuckoldry. If the cuckold was of the noble grades, for example, and the real father a *dóer*, how could the latter pay the huge fee in compensation? The reverse was even more serious. The honour-price and so on of the *dóer* was so low that a nobleman could have all the fun he wished for very little penalty. The lawyers endeavoured to go around the difficulties by bringing up the price in the latter case until it equalled what might be expected from a wealthier man. When a poorer man has cuckolded a richer one, he must endeavour to pay the whole compensation. When he cannot do so, his son shall pay later out of the property he has from his richer reputed father.

The dilemma of a man with regard to the paternity of a child is well and enigmatically expressed by some old Gaelic poet and it is quoted by the brehon laws: *Saer brú beiris breith/do thabairt clí* – 'the fertile womb is free to bear a body!' No matter what rule or law may decree, it can happen that the woman may have a child for anyone who takes her fancy. Laws and decrees cannot rule her fertility.[2]

In practice the man who suspected cuckoldry of himself did not often wait for his wife to bear the child or even to become pregnant in order to obtain his own kind of natural satisfaction for his humiliation, real or supposed. One of the most famous stories of the early Irish period is that of the Madness of Sweeney, a king who lost both kingdom, wife and reason after the Battle of Moira in 637 AD. Ever after this Sweeney became a mad refugee in the woods of Ireland. He spent most of a year being fed secretly by a swineherd's wife. Poor Sweeney was duly grateful and did not molest the girl or have a love-affair with her. Then she was seen by another woman meeting Sweeney and was accused by her of cuckolding her husband. The swineherd was told of this and he followed her one morning, with the reproach of the woman in his ear: 'Your woman is with another man over there in the fence, you effeminate weakling!' He saw Sweeney on the ground near his wife drinking milk from a hollow in cowdung (!) and pierced him through the breast, severing his spinal cord and condemning him to a slow death. Too late he found out how wrong he was.[3] This story must surely re-echo what happened in cases of adultery or of cuckoldry in these times, whatever wise provisions the brehon laws had made for peaceful settlement.

ABDUCTION

Although the children of abduction had no slur attached to them and were 'legitimate' according to the brehon laws, the matter had to be regulated carefully. The sober law-tracts set before us between the lines the scene of abduction: The woman may be taken into a wood by her abductor. She may be carried on horseback across the open plain. She may also be transported across a river boundary in a boat. It is stated that any relative of the woman or anyone in a position of responsibility in the *tuath*, who is witness to the abduction, must report it and make a complaint within twenty-four hours. If there is no witness to the abduction among those mentioned already, ten days grace are given within which an objection can be raised by those responsible for the welfare of the girl. It appears that the reason for this was that it might take this length of time for the news to percolate through to them from a public assembly, such as a fair, or some other meeting place where the news of the country would be swopped.[4]

Whoever sought a woman for himself by abduction had to pay rather dearly for it. By taking the woman in this manner he had avoided all the formal property arrangements which were the norm. In fact he had taken a short cut, spurred on by greed or perhaps desire, to get all he wanted for nothing. In later times he would have had the woman easily. The fear of dishonour would make her parents come to heel in an effort to stave off the slur on the family. It was different in the Ireland of the brehon laws.

In laying down norms for dealing with a case of abduction the brehon lawyers took two important factors into consideration. The first was whether the girl was taken against her will or voluntarily. The other factor was whether she had been brought to some place within the *tuath* or outside the jurisdiction. At this point it should be noted that both the brehon laws and the whole cultural system of ancient Ireland were commonly observed throughout all the country, even though there were a very large number of autonomous regions, the *tuaths*.

Wherever the abduction was against the girl's will, the culprit was obliged to pay the girl her honour-price first of all. This seems reasonable because such a mating could hardly be more than a fleeting affair. Then he also must pay her relatives and the chief men of the *tuath* their honour-prices. If she dies outside the jurisdiction of the *tuath* he must also pay body-price for her and honour-price for her kindred. In the case of a girl forcibly cohabited with while she is living in the *tuath*, her kindred must still receive body and honour-prices if she dies in childbirth. If, however, she dies within the jurisdiction of natural causes other than childbirth, the abductor is exempt from any penalties for her death.

In the case of a voluntary abduction, or elopement, as we would call it nowadays, the case is different. Her relatives and the heads of her kindred receive both body and honour-prices but she receives nothing. If she dies of any cause outside the jurisdiction within the space of a month, her kindred must be paid both body-and honour-prices.

When we come to consider the law regarding the child born to the abducted girl, we can see how the ancient laws safeguarded the position of such a child in society. First of all, any child conceived within a month of the abduction belongs to the mother's people. They then have the right to sell such a child. When the buyer has paid what is judged right, the child is then accorded the status of a *cétmuinter's* child (the progeny of a first-contract wife) or the status of another contracted partner who succeeds a *cétmuinter* child (the progeny of a first-contracted wife) or the status of another contracted partner who succeeds a *cétmuinter* after a divorce. To use the British legal term, all children of an abducted girl were officially legitimised. One should stress at this point that the brehon laws were considering the case of a girl got with child in a situation which we might really call rape: where force was used the mother's people had a choice of either selling the child or rearing it themselves. If the child is sold, the father is obliged to buy it. In the case of the girl consenting to what he did, he has a choice of either buying the child or not.[5]

ADULTERY

When we come to speak of adultery a clear-cut distinction should be made between the case of someone starting a steady relationship with the new woman and a fleeting affair. The sign of serious intent was when the lover gave the woman a *coibche*. Whenever a woman received this formal sign of interest in her, the man must give his *cétmuinter* back her *coibche*, as well as her honour-price. There is also the case considered of the woman who decides to stay on in the house when her husband has taken on the new woman. Then she must receive additional compensation as well.[6]

The new partner had to pay for her freshly won position. She must give her rival what she has received from her lover and then also pay her an honour-price.[7]

Reference has already been made to what Geoffrey Keating says regarding the *coibche*. He saw it as a present made to the girl by a king when he wished to sleep with her. In another manuscript we hear of the conception of the early Irish king, Cormac Mac Airt, who is supposed to have lived in the third century of the Christian era. His father, Art, was on his way to the battle where he fell. He stayed the night with a smith, to whose daughter he gave a *coibche*. He slept with her that night and Cormac was born of the encounter.[8]

Legislating for human nature, the brehon laws made due provision for a woman whose man has committed adultery. If his wife is a *cétmuinter*, who has not got a legal separation from him, she has protection from the ancient laws for acts of jealousy. For three days she has total exemption from penalties for both minor and major offences against his person and the person of his new love. This means that all crimes up to blood-letting, as well as serious assault, are exempt! It behoved a husband in these times to keep himself and his paramour clear of his wife unless he had taken the necessary legal steps to get rid of her beforehand! After three days the wife is exempt from half the penalties for both minor and major offences for a month. This depends totally on whether she is still his legal partner, as before, and also on whether his wife has taken another man. If she has, she loses the exemption.

Any other woman who holds the status of wife is granted exemption for three days from minor offences against the person of a rival woman and her husband. Similarly for the rest of the month she is exempt from half the penalties for minor offences. All this exemption depends on whether he has got a separation from her husband and/or has gone to live with another man.[9]

There is a story told about Cormac Mac Airt which might be recalled here. It is said that a band of Ulstermen raided Scotland and took a large number of people captive home to Ireland. Among them was Ciarnait, the daughter of the King of the Picts of Scotland. She was a very lovely girl and Cormac Mac Airt heard of her. He succeeded in buying her and then became her lover. Cormac's wife became jealous of the girl. Instead of lowering her dignity by assaulting and perhaps killing a rival, the queen demanded that she be given her as a slave for her own use. She then compelled the girl to grind a large amount of corn each day. In spite of that the lovers continued to meet and she became pregnant. Cormac was filled with sympathy for the burden of work laid on his loved one. He sent to Scotland for a mason who knew how to construct a water-mill to spare the girl from what she had to do hitherto by hand on a quern. It is said that in this way a water-mill was first built in Ireland. It is significant that it was built to spare a pregnant girl from undue toil.[10]

In the foregoing short account of how matters such as cuckoldry, adultery and abduction fitted into ancient Irish society, the concern of the brehon laws was always to pro-tect the woman and the child against the predations of men or, in the case of cuckoldry, to protect a husband against another man's interest. The general objects of the laws in these matters as in everything else was to arrange things in dispute according to some principle which took full ac-count of human propensity, recognise the accomplished fact, and use a form of arbitration and composition for the settlement of crimes and misdemeanours instead of jailing and punishing the wrong-doer physically. One must see the laws in operation as a method of treating each person as a member of a family or co-family group, for whom the heads of such a group was responsible. They acted to-gether and met the representatives of the other side in a dispute. One feels that this may have been much better than treating each malefactor as an individual, who must fend for himself. For certain serious crimes a person could indeed be made an outcast – a *deorad* – one who is de-prived of the protection of his kin. His lot was a bad one and, unless he could atone for his crimes, a hopeless one.

WOMEN OUTSIDE THE LAW[1]

The brehons reckoned that there were seven grades of women who could not have compensation levied on their behalf if they were raped or surreptitiously cohabited with. They were not accounted 'good women' and the tract mentions that they were, according to the old saying, like the women of Lismore! Why the ladies of Lismore in early Ireland earned this reputation, one is not told.

i) The first type of woman for whose violation a man could not be held accountable before the law was the prostitute who offered her body to every man who paid her.

ii) The next type of woman mentioned is she who is being cohabited with surreptitiously, e.g., while she is sleeping, and does not make any attempt to resist or protest when she becomes aware of what is happening.

iii) We next hear of a woman who conceals the fact that she has been raped until some time after the event. With her is placed she who is raped in a habitation area (*cathair*) and does not call out for aid until her violator has made his escape.

iv) The fourth woman who, as it were, loses any right to have proceedings initiated on her behalf for sexual offences committed against her is one who announces that she will violate her fidelity to her husband.

v) The fifth case is that of the woman who makes an arrangement with a man to meet him in a 'bush or a bed', as the laws picturesquely put it. She has definitely consented to what happened and her husband cannot claim any fines on her behalf.

vi) The woman who requests a cleric to enjoy her bodily pleasures is also counted among the number.

vii) The last case mentioned is that of the woman who offers herself to a man on difficult conditions. Actually a gloss states that this means offering herself on unusual or non-customary *coibche*-terms. This hard-bargaining is presumed to have lost her her rights of redress before the law if she is raped or fraudulently slept with.

DIVORCE

To THOSE BROUGHT UP with the misleading notion that modern Ireland is somehow the heir of the ancient Gaelic system, it sometimes comes as a surprise to hear that divorce was recognised and practised in the times of the brehon laws. The laws, as we know them, were written in Christian times and frequent references to the Church confirms this. Nevertheless, in spite of monk and priest, the most that the continental religion could do was to have a man's *cétmuinter* recognised as his chief wife with special position and privileges not accorded to anyone else. So strong was the old tradition of freedom in marital matters that the laws regarding separation with the right of contracting another sexual partnership legally were never changed. It took the Norman Conquest of the twelfth century to bring the acceptance of the divorceless marriage to Ireland and the final collapse of the old Gaelic system in the sixteenth century to have it enforced throughout the country. The modern Irish state, born out of the Irish Literary Renascence and Gaelic Revival of the beginning of this century, turned out to be a poor version of the most narrow-minded Victorian attitudes imaginable. In this situation the women suffered the most by deprivation of rights with no hope of redress. Furthermore, they were conditioned to accept their lot as just until the later years of the twentieth century when legal separation was recognised and legislated for and where, at long last, a referendum on divorce was passed, albeit with a tiny majority in 1995. The referendum result was unsuccessfully challenged in the courts. In 1916–1923 their men fought for freedom. The women did not attain full freedom in a sociological sense until the last two decades of the twentieth century.

It is rather important, therefore, to see what the brehon laws offered to couples whose marriages had become unsatisfactory. The word 'become' is used advisedly. Human development varies from person to person and time may change some basic traits in the character of either husband or wife, or in both, so that the well-matched couple of the wedding-day may become in time the ill-met partners whose only hope of happiness may be in a proper legal separation with freedom to remarry. This fact has been denied by priests, some of whom may know little about marriage except what they hear in the confessional or from gossiping trouble-makers.

GROUNDS FOR SEPARATION

Two categories of people were distinguished by the brehons where this matter of separation or divorce was concerned. In the first category the departing one did not incur any penalties or have to pay any special compensation to the woman he is leaving, except the natural division of property and wealth, which will be discussed further on in this chapter. The second category is that of women who have acquired a right to divorce their husbands and be fully compensated in all respects for their trouble.

Here are what might be called the 'no-fault' divorce-grounds:

i) If illness has made the marriage impossible and also if separation is necessary due to some disease.

ii) Pilgrimage being made by one of the parties: in this case one can see the influence of the Christian religion excusing from penalty the one going away.

iii) Some serious physical blemish or injury, which is not cured or curable, in the opinion of a brehon, a physician or a nobleman.

iv) Leaving the territory to seek a friend or avenge an aggression or any such reason. The general notion here is that the absence is likely to be prolonged or perpetual.

v) Loss of sanity.

vi) If the parties are barren, they may separate without penalty in order to form another union or unions to have children.

vii) The laws also add 'death' as another reason. This was necessary to cover the case of the other partner claiming penalties against the kindred of the deceased one.[1]

The second category of those who may separate with full compensation, so to speak, and who have the right to go whenever they like, taking their *coibche* with them, are the following seven types of women:

i) A woman whose husband circulates a false story about her among the people. In other words, serious vilification of his wife by a husband automatically gives her right of separation.

ii) If her husband circulates a satire about his wife which makes her a laughing-stock among her neighbours and acquaintances, she can leave him without blame to herself. Note how this and the preceding case arise out of the proud and sensitive Irish character.

iii) Any woman who has been struck a blow which blemishes her, is also entitled to separation without blame to herself. In this case it is not quite clear whether the blow should be one which leaves a permanent blemish or just one which leaves a mark which is healable.[2]

iv) A woman who is repudiated for another.

v) The woman who is deprived of sexual intercourse by her husband. The tract mentions in this case that the husband prefers the company of servant-boys when this is not necessary for him. Evidently this is a reference to a homosexual cohabitation when the man has a wife who desires him. In such a case she has a right to a divorce.

vi) If a husband gives his wife a philtre – a charm of some kind – to induce her to sleep with him, this forms grounds for divorce on her side.

vii) A woman who is not given what she desires in

54

food and such like things may rightfully divorce her husband without blame.[3]

In addition to all these cases mentioned above, there were also those already quoted in Chapter 2 in the list of those men who could not legally contract a marriage. In some of these cases, e.g., impotence and barrenness, the other partner may have been deceived before marriage or else a genuine error may have been made. In all such cases a divorce was allowable. It should be noted that possibly every reason for a dissolution of a marriage was foreseen and legislated for.

It is noteworthy that the woman who flees from her marital contract, i.e., who does so without sufficient cause, is classed with such people as a wandering thief, one who has committed murder, those who have fled from maintaining father or mother and a fugitive from his kindred. All these have the same disability in common. They have no protection under the brehon laws.[4]

PRINCIPLES OF SEPARATION

The one thing that the brehon laws sought in the separation was that the wife was not defrauded of her property. It should be mentioned that there was no divorce court to which the couple could be summoned, where all their intimate affairs might be blazoned forth for the public to regale itself with. The matter was decided first between the couple, and then the business arrangements were made regarding the division of property.

If a woman separates from her husband without sufficient reason, in other words, if it can be shown that she is to blame for the breakup of the marriage, she must return all the *coibche* presents she received from him, and her kindred must also do the same. If the marriage had lasted a considerable time, this could amount to a considerable figure, because a *coibche* was paid out each year of marriage up to the twenty-first by the husband. In the case of separation for any reason, the chief of the kindred of the woman must return his share of the *coibche* to the husband.[5] In other cases, where the husband is to blame for the ending of the marriage contract, the whole *coibche* in the possession of the woman is kept by her.

It should also be stated that the arrangements which will be given in some detail below are a minimum. Such penalties as honour-price and body-price and so on, may also be levied on the husband if he has committed adultery openly and brought another woman into the house without getting a legal separation first of all.

SEPARATION OF EQUAL PARTNERS

Since the 'normal' marriage was one of equal partners, the 'normal' type of separation is between two such people and is carefully treated in the brehon laws. The question of who should have the custody of the children did not arise at all. They were in fosterage from their infancy and had been provided for by the parents from that time, as has been pointed out already. This fact eliminated a very sensitive point indeed, if one reads the accounts of divorce-suits and the bitter disputes which arise concerning the ultimate disposal of the children when a couple separate nowadays.

The tract dealing with separation proclaims that every such separation should be without fraud, and if they are separating of their own free will and choice, they should divide their property in a lawful manner. The general principle laid down was that applying to the increase in property such as cattle, pigs and corn. What the woman still had of what she owned when she first married, was her own naturally. This she took. As to the produce of animals one-third of the increase was left behind on the land, another third went to the owner of the cattle, and the last third was divided in three and given to the husband, departing wife and herdsmen in equal shares. In practice, if she, for example, had sixty-three animals born to her cows while she was married, she took twenty-one and an additional seven for attendance or service. In this way the claims of the occupier of the land – the husband – were met adequately.[6]

The all-important business of the division of the milk was next decided by the lawyers. In this case one should read 'butter' for milk. During the season of high milk-yield – the time of booleying from May until November – the butter was stored in wooden kegs and hidden in moist or swampy ground. A threefold division was also made between the owner of the land, the owner of the cows and those who have worked at the care of the animals and making of butter. The last third was subdivided as follows: one half went to the woman, and the other fraction was divided among the owners of the vessels, the husband and the other workers (a complicated division of one-twelfth, one-eighteenth and one-thirty-sixth).[7]

When the separation is due to the woman taking another man, she loses her right to share the part of the last 'service' third but otherwise can claim the other proportions of the division of animals or butter mentioned above.[8]

When the laws treat of corn or bacon, they speak of the 'service' third alone. Of this third she claims one third, if she has looked after the ploughing and reaping, fed the workmen, and saw to it that the pigs were fattened. The last item refers to seeing to it that they were herded properly in the forests. If she fed them with milk, however, she can claim two-thirds for service and attendance. It should be noted that this seems to refer to pigs not her own property. Of the spring service she received two-thirds; the reason seems to have been that the woman had the care of the workmen and the swineherds in the farrowing season to an extent which might not occur later in the year.[9]

When it came to the division of wool and the dye-plant *(glaisín)* which was used, the position was as follows: the woman could take as her own one half of whatever cloth she had woven or of the wool she had spun while married. She was entitled to one-third of the wool which has been combed once and a sixth of the wool which is in locks or sheaves of flax. As to the dye-plant, she received one-third of it at a preliminary stage of preparation and one half if it be fully prepared for use.[10]

Everything belonging to one of the separating parties, which has been consumed or used up by the other, must be restituted.[11] In the case of theft, open or secret, and violent seizure, restitution must be made doubly with the increase, i.e., calves with their mothers.[12]

The wife gets one-ninth of the corn sown and reaped by the husband, and one-ninth of the bacon, if she is a hard worker. The usual method of settling her claims to corn, apparently, was to give her a sack of corn for every month of the year she had been with him before separation. The year for this purpose was described as stretching from May-Day to May-Day.[13] On this day each year the women, children and herdsmen set out for the summer pasturages – the booleys – and stayed there until the first day of November. Tillage was attended to around the homestead when the animals were out of the way.

When the marriage had been one where the man was supported on the woman's property, suitable arrangements were made with the man set in the woman's place, as described above.[14]

The case of the man who has been frequenting the company of a woman was also provided for. He is seen as the lover who does not have the ordinary business and service relationships with her. In this case, however, he has a right to one-fifth of her hand-produce, i.e., cloth, wool and the life.[15]

The laws also consider the case of the woman who has been abducted and who wishes to separate from her man. In this case, there is no division of property but the woman takes away with her anything which she has brought and the man has no right to anything she has whatsoever.[16]

The marriage brought about by force or secrecy is next considered. In this case no property arrangements have been made and the man has to pay the usual penalties mentioned in Chapter 3. Another aspect of the matter is noticed too: if the girl who has been forced or violated is in her second stage of life – between seven and twelve years of age (!) – the man must pay a full *éraic* in compensation, the so-called blood-money, the penalty inflicted on the murderer. This applies also to a girl who has taken the nun's veil and when a *cétmuinter* is the victim. In the case of any other woman the special fine is half the *éraic*.[17]

The last case of divorce and separation to be considered is that of the marriage of two idiots or lunatics. If there is a child born of this union, the care of fosterage falls on whoever united the couple for fun or as a practical joke. This person must also answer for their crimes and misdemeanours and be their security before the law. His sense of humour could cost him dear before he is finished with the whole business![18] We gather from the legal tract that a marriage was solemnised before one person, at least.

When reading through the brehon laws one is interested in the fact that all types of separation were noted. For example, the situation of the forced girl was considered. As should be remembered, the ten types of social relationships for procreation as mentioned in Chapter 2, cover well-nigh all circumstances under which a man and a woman might cohabit together. Throughout the laws there is no talk of the sacred character of marriage. Any such character cannot really come from the formal binding together of a couple; it must grow. Marriage, therefore, was a relative thing. Its success depended on time, place and persons concerned. It was no absolute thing in the eyes of the brehons, who were human beings legislating for human beings, and not idealists legislating like God.

This was the strength and humanity of these laws of ancient Ireland.

An Extra-Marital Adventure

It can be claimed for artistic expression of any kind that it gets to the heart of things and illustrates the way of human nature better than a thousand definitions and many precise tomes of scholarship. Having dealt with the laws concerning divorce in early Ireland, it seems that we should now look at one of the Ulster saga tales, which centres around Cuchulainn, called *The Wasting Sickness of Cuchulainn and The One Jealousy of Emer*.[1] The tale, as told here, is found in the manuscript called *The Book of the Dun Cow*, written in Clonmacnoise in the middle of the eleventh century. Both the language of this tale (adapted from Old Irish), its theme and its general atmosphere suggest that it is very old indeed; older than the eleventh century, at all events. It reflects, therefore, attitudes and emotions in early Ireland with the more ancient elements covered lightly by an overlay from the eleventh century.

This story is really an evocation of the hero Cuchulainn's boredom with his wife, Emer, and his affair with a beautiful lady of the other world. It does not end in divorce but in reconciliation with his wife.

The story begins in *Samhain*, the great pre-winter festival in the beginning of November. The chief men of Ulster and their wives have come together for the festival and Cuchulainn and his wife are also there. Cuchulainn is requested by the women to kill birds for them with his sling and he does this with his usual unerring skill. Then Conor Mac Nessa's wife asks him to kill two birds who are approaching linked together by a golden chain. He endeavours repeatedly to strike them down but fails. This upsets him so much that he sits at the foot of a pillar-stone

61

and falls into a deep sleep of depression and humiliation. His failure to satisfy a woman had unmanned him, as it were.

As Cuchulainn sits there, he is approached by two women, one dressed in a green and the other in a purple cloak. They smile at him and then horsewhip him unmercifully. This sadistic beating almost kills him. After this his companions carry him to his house and he remains there for a year without speaking a word to anyone, even to his wife, Emer. Up to this point in the story there seems to be a symbolic representation of a man's boredom with his former heterosexual relationship with his wife.

At the end of the year Cuchulainn is visited by a person from the *síd* or fairy otherworld. After this visit Cuchulainn speaks and tells of his experience with the two flagellators at the pillar-stone on the previous *Samhain*. He asks Conor Mac Nessa for advice and is told to return to the scene of the beating. This time he is approached by the green-cloaked lady. She informs him that the king of the otherworld's daughter, Fand, loves him. She is sought as wife by three enemies of her people but desires only Cuchulainn.

Cuchulainn sends his charioteer to see Fand's country – *Mág Mell* – the Elysium of the ancient Gaels. They travel in a bronze boat over the sea and after the visit the charioteer returns to report to his master. Cuchulainn then sends the charioteer to Emer to inform her that fairy-women have come to allure him. Then Emer reproaches the charioteer for allowing her husband to waste away with the sickness which has lain on him for more than a year. She also reproves the men of Ulster for not helping their champion in his hour of need. He had always been at their service, she points out, and they should have ministered to him when he needed them. She then went to see Cuchulainn.

When she arrived at the house where her husband was staying, we are told that she sat on the couch where he lay and said: 'It is a disgrace for you that you are unable to make love to a woman'. In vain she endeavours to arouse him from his lassitude. He is beyond her aid now.

Afterwards he arises and travels to a place where he once more meets the green-cloaked lady. He informs her that he has no intention of visiting her country at a woman's invitation! Once more the charioteer is sent there as his master's emissary and he meets Fand. Fand changes her tactics and, instead of issuing an invitation to Cuchulainn to be her lover, she lets him know that she needs his help as a warrior. This fetches him. He travels to her and kills her three unwelcome suitors in battle. His strength and skill now return to him and his battle-rage becomes so great that he must be cooled afterwards in three vats of water!

Fand greets her victorious hero afterwards with what is a wooing song. She chants:

> Welcome, Cuchulainn!
> Pursuing boar!
> Great warrior of Muirheimne Plain!
> Great is his spirit!
> Highest of battle-winning heroes!
> Heart of a warrior!
> Battle-stone of wisdom!
> Blood-redness of anger!
> Ready for enemies!
> Ulster's brave warrior!
> Beautiful his splendour!
> Splendour to women's eyes!
> And welcome!

After this he made love to Fand and remained with her for a month. He then returned home to Ulster having agreed to an assignation with her near Newry. He came back rejuvenated by his experience.

Emer heard this. She became furiously jealous and had knives made for her retinue of fifty girls to attack Fand when she arrived in Ireland to meet Cuchulainn. The hero was calmly playing chess with his charioteer and Fand had already come, when Emer and her knife-packing ladies came in sight. They were travelling in chariots. So engrossed was Cuchulainn in his chess-game, that it was Fand who noticed the visitors and she drew the charioteer's attention to them. Then Emer faced Cuchulainn and a dialogue took place between them which is vibrant with the clash of emotions between the husband and a betrayed and jealous wife.

'I don't fear you nor your hosts either!' remarked Cuchulainn with sarcasm, when he saw the armed women. He continued: 'You came in a powerful chariot on a splendid seat before my very eyes, so that I may rescue you from the many maidens of the four corners of Ireland! What will Forgall's daughter (Emer) threaten to do because of my actions? This is something which I will not tolerate.'

After this outburst from the angry man she did not reply. Then he continued: 'I'm avoiding attacking you, woman, as anyone avoids attacking a friend. I'm neither cutting down your frail thin knife with a steel javelin nor your cowardly anger.' He then added: 'I find it extremely difficult to unyoke my strength from that of a woman.' (This last statement played on the second meaning of the word for 'strength', which is 'sexual potency'.)

After this firm statement Emer turned away from her futile display of aggression and asked: 'I have a question for you: What caused you, Cuchulainn, to dishonour me before all the girls of the province and of Ireland? And before all people of standing?' Having asked this question as so many have done before her time and since, she continued in anger: 'I'm here under your protection and guardianship. You're not threatened by quarrelsome pride but perchance you won't succeed in leaving me, lad, although you're attempting to do so.'

Cuchulainn then counters this with a reply which might make little sense nowadays in such an encounter but which would have appeared completely reasonable under the brehon laws, which allowed concubines.

'I have a question for you, Emer!' he retorted. 'Why don't you allow me to spend time with a woman? First of all, she is a woman who is clean, chaste (i.e., attached to one man), bright, clever, sprightly; the daughter of a king from overseas, of fair aspect and good nation. She can do handicraft and manufacture. She has understanding, intelligence and strength of mind. She has many horses and herds, so that there is not under heaven anything which she wouldn't do for her lover, even though you'd promise it. Emer, you'll find no wound-giving warrior that is as good as I.'

The foregoing speech makes little sense unless we understand that he was presuming on his right to a concubine, as he was entitled, and also that he was pointing out to Emer that his loved one was not just a cheap tramp but a fine and noble lady. Evidently, this was less of an insult to his wife than if he took an unworthy woman! Another comment that can be added to this speech is that he was indulging in a welter of self-praise, as his concluding words prove.

Emer retorted to this male chauvinism with a penetrating remark on the attitude of a straying husband to his new love.

'I suppose, the woman you're following,' she began sardonically with a reference to her own arrival, armed and in a chariot, 'is not a charioteer! However, each red thing is beautiful, each new thing is fine, each height is pleasant, each commonplace thing is disagreeable, each want is revered, and all that's familiar is neglected, until everything becomes known! At one time, lad, we were held in high esteem by you and would be again, if you wish!' The storyteller then adds: 'And she was sad.' She then pronounced: 'Upon my word! This is a sore business for me and will also be so for you while you live!

Fand had been standing silently listening to all this dialogue but now she intervened with an outburst: 'Let me have him!'

'More rightly, I should have him!' Emer retorted.

'No!' said Fand. 'It's I has more right to him because I was put at risk a while ago!' After this reference to the knife-bearing Emer and her maidens, she felt she was defeated and became upset and depressed, because she did not wish to leave her lover and suffer the humiliation of having to return unwanted and alone to her house. Emer won back her errant husband and we hear that Mannanán Mac Lir, the god of the sea, appeared and rescued Fand from the predicament in which she had found herself.

This extraordinary story recreates the situation of a husband who is bored with his wife and goes into a state of depression and what the story calls 'wasting sickness'. Then he is led into the arms of another woman who leads him to her by calling on him to use his skills in a good cause. He becomes revitalised and, as they say, a new man, and returns from the adventure a better person. This type of theme scarcely fits into any kind of bourgeois morality or moralising known to us.

This short chapter should also contain some account of a most charming story from early Ireland of the unconquerable and persistent love of a man and a woman for each other. Their love persisted beyond death and through three existences, until it was finally consummated. It is the tale of the beautiful and mythical lady, Étaín. This story is an expression of the theme of unconquerable and irresistible love as the early Irish people saw it.

The king, Midir, had a wife named Fuamnach. To Fuamnach's fury her husband fell in love with the beautiful Étaín and they became lovers. Fuamnach made use of magical powers which turned her rival into a pool of water and when the water evaporated in the heat of the sun, a worm appeared in it. This worm became a butterfly and Fuamnach became enraged by the attention which the butterfly paid to her husband and had it driven by a wind throughout the country for seven years.

Étaín's misery found a temporary relief when she was blown into the house of Aengus, who always went about with three birds around him. These birds were his kisses and all those who heard their song fell in love with Aengus and could not resist him. Aengus desired Étaín and succeeded in transforming her from dusk till dawn. By night he was her lover; by day he kept her in a crystal sun-house where she was surrounded by the fragrance of flowers.

Meanwhile two people were seeking her. Fuamnach sought her to destroy her and Midir to take her to himself again. Fuamnach found her first and blew her away. She found herself in the house of the king of Ulster, fell into the drinking vessel of the queen, and was swallowed by her. She was reincarnated in the womb of the queen and born once more.

When Étaín grew up in her new existence, she became once more the beautiful creature which she had been before. The King of Tara at this time was seeking a wife and, when he discovered the Ulster king's daughter, Étaín, he married her. Midir was still seeking her and a number of times he approached in disguise and asked her to become his lover. She refused without first asking her husband's consent and this Midir knew would not be given.

Then Midir came openly to her husband and played chess with him. He lost the first two games and paid his stake but won the third one. His stake this time was one kiss from Étaín. Her husband reluctantly agreed and settled a day one month later when Midir could come and kiss his wife. One might surmise here that the word 'kiss' is a euphemism for love-making. At all events the jealous husband had the house surrounded by armed men to take and

kill Midir after he had received what he had won. Étaín
during the month had recalled her former existence and
her love and longing for Midir returned. When he came to
her and received the satisfaction of his stake, he held Étaín
in a tight embrace and both rose through the roof of the
house as two swans and flew away safely from the swords
of those awaiting Midir.

THE CHRISTIAN CHURCH

AT SOME STAGE DURING the fourth or fifth century the Christian Church was established in Ireland. It does not concern us here how this came about, whether it was carried out due to the ministry of one St Patrick or more.

Ireland had escaped Roman domination and with the advent of the Christian Church the people were exposed to a system of ecclesiastical law which was based on Roman legal practice. In fact, the brehon laws were radically different in many respects from the laws of the new religion which came from Britain and the European continent and there was bound to be some conflict between the two. The interesting and, perhaps, extraordinary thing about the Church in Ireland up to the coming of the Normans was that brehon law practice and Church law co-existed in such sensitive areas as those concerning marriage and sex. It has been pointed out already that the most that the Church could force the brehon lawyers to do in these areas was to give a special status to the *cétmuinter* – the first contracted wife. This and the use of the term *ben adaltrach* (literally 'adulteress') as a title for any other marital partner or concubine which a man might take, seem to have been the limit of the Church's influence.

It evidently took a while for the Church to gain enough influence to exert its authority in the country and the ecclesiastical documents which are extant chart the growth and scope of this. One document, which is worthy of note is described as the 'Synod of St Patrick'.[1] It is a circular letter composed by Patrick, Auxilius and Iserninus, all foreign missionaries of the fifth century, which calls the attention of the new Christian flock to certain points which needed observance. These points which deal with the subject of this book shed some light on the Ireland of the fifth century. Consider the following:

i) A Christian who has committed ... adultery ... shall do a year's penance for (it); the year of penance completed, he shall come and be absolved by a priest, when he has brought witnesses of his penance.

ii) Any virgin, vowed to chastity, who takes a lover, shall be excommunicated until she is converted. After her conversion and her dismissal of the adulterer, she shall do penance and afterwards must not live in the same house or village as he.

iii) Any woman who has taken a man in a decent marriage and who leaves him to go with an adulter is excommunicated. This is a direct blow at the tolerant custom permitted under the brehon laws.

iv) If any man gives his daughter in a decent marriage and if she then loves another man, and he consents and accepts a dowry for her, both shall be shut out from the Church. Here we have an echo of the father accepting a *coibche* for any daughter who is married or remarried.

v) Any cleric from ostiary to priest, who is seen without a tunic and does not cover the shame or nakedness of his body, and whose hair is not barbered in the Roman manner, and whose wife walks about with her head uncovered, shall be despised by the laity and separated from the Church. This particular ordinance refers to the fact that celibacy was not enjoined on the early clerics of the Christian Church in Ireland. The celibates among the clerics at this stage in Irish ecclesiastical history were the monks and their counterparts, the nuns.

vi) A monk and a virgin from separate places shall not lodge in the same hostelry nor travel in the same chariot from village to village nor carry on continual conversations with each other.

These ordinances are simply the first onset by the

Christian Church on the society formed by the tolerant brehon laws.

THE HOLY FINNIAN

There were two abbots named Finnian who lived in the sixth century and one of these holy gentlemen was the author of a penitential which is still extant. A penitential is a listing of sins, and the penances deemed fitting for them. A reading of Finnian's Penitential opens one's eyes to how matters had progressed since the beginning of established Christianity in Ireland, a century, at most.[2]

The merciless tone of this penitential is evident from such an ordinance as that which deals with adultery. If any man makes love to his neighbour's wife or daughter, he has a year's penance on bread and water awaiting him. In addition to this he is forbidden to make love to his own wife. One wonders how effective all this rigour was.

There is a section in this penitential devoted to the use of magic in sexual matters. It is specifically stated that if a cleric or a woman, who are practising magic should lead anyone astray by the magic, this is to be punished by six years penance. Three of these years are on bread and water and the other three are penitential years when neither wine nor meat may be taken. Magic is regarded as a 'monstrous sin'. The person who gives a potion so as to arouse sexual love, is condemned to one year's bread and water. It may come as a surprising echo of these times to read next that any woman who kills the child within her by magic earns for herself half a year of bread and water fast, two years abstention from wine and meat and in this last period she has six forty-day stretches of bread and water fast.

This last paragraph applies to nuns. The penitential goes on to state what should be done in the case of a nun who bears a child. She must spend six years on bread and water. After the conclusion of her penance she is once more ceremoniously clothed in white and declared a virgin.

Having dealt with the nun, the penitential turns to her lover. The layman who performs the deed from which the child is begotten, is condemned to three years of penance. In the first year he is on bread and water and is not allowed to sleep with his wife; in the second period of two years, he may not take meat or wine and is again prohibited from sleeping with his wife. It should be remarked here that the brehon laws allow a separation to any woman whose husband has not cohabited with her. One regrets the paucity of records for enlightenment on what exactly happened in practice in cases such as this.

The penitential in detail next goes on to the case of the fellow who makes love to a nun but without a resultant pregnancy. This lad earns himself one year's bread and water and half a year's abstention from wine and meat. He is also forbidden to have intercourse with his wife during all this time.

The penitential of Finnian considers the case of a man who seeks separation and remarriage on the grounds of the barrenness of his wife. This, it should be recalled, provided grounds for a divorce in the brehon law system. Finnian has something else to say. Let them, says he, remain continent, and they are happy if they remain chaste of body until God gives true and just judgment on them! In other words, they must stay together until death. Note that the woman bears the blame!

Turning to another matter – the case of a woman who has left her husband to go and live with another man and who is allowed legal separation under the brehon laws – Finnian forbids the deserted husband to remarry while his wife still lives. If she returns to him, he is instructed not to make any payment to her but she must compensate him. Here, evidently, is a reference to the law which would have regarded her return as a new contract requiring the payment of a *coibche* by the husband. The case of the women sent away by the husband receives the same type of cold comfort. She is to live in chastity until such time as he repents and takes her back. In all cases, such as those mentioned in this paragraph, the couple must abstain for a year from intercourse as a penance. One wonders what real knowledge of human nature these good saints, such as Finnian, had.

Not content with legislating for the social contract of marriage, Finnian then lays down rules for the marriage bed. He orders that all couples should abstain from sex for three forty-day periods each year. As well as this, they are to abstain on Saturday and Sunday nights and also during pregnancy.

There is also a penitential which was written by Columbanus, the monk from Bangor.[3] This probably dates from the seventh century. Columbanus was a missionary who founded monasteries in France, Switzerland and Italy and who numbered among his enemies kings, queens, fellow-monks and one of the popes of the era. He was ferocious in his penitential severity and uncompromising when dealing with human emotions whenever they ran counter to his notions of what was good. The monastic rule which he spread throughout Europe gave way before the Benedictines, principally because it was so severe and inhuman that the moderate Rule of Benedict was preferred to it. Columbanus did not heed in his Irish extremist attitude what a normal man could endure reasonably in a lifetime in a monastery; Benedict did most admirably. Typical of the penances and general attitudes found in the Columban penitential is the following: anyone committing fornication once only is condemned to three years of penance; for more frequent fun of the same kind he is to do seven years! For anyone 'fornicating as the Sodomites did' there is ten years penance; the first three on bread and water and during the other seven he must abstain from wine and meat. Going further the holy Columbanus turns on anyone who has made use of magic to arouse love. This person faces a year of penance, if he is a cleric; if he is a layman he has half a year! There was little pity or understanding in the Columban system.

THE CANONS OF THE ALLEGED SYNOD OF ST PATRICK

A very interesting document is that containing the decrees of some synod of the Irish Church which may have been held in the seventh century.[4] This collection has been called the Canons of St Patrick's Second Synod; erroneously, it appears. It is worthwhile looking at them and comparing what they contain on matters of marriage and sexual mores with what appears in the decrees of the circular letter almost certainly issued in the time of Patrick and his companions.

The Christian people are forcibly reminded that a 'prostitute wife' is a harlot who deserves stoning as an adulteress, according to the Mosaic Law. To make the matter clear, it pointed out that remarriage after a wife's death is allowed. Thus the canons are attacking directly the tolerance of the brehon laws which allowed separation and remarriage.

The authority of the father in choosing a husband for his daughter is upheld but it is also reasonably stipulated that the girl's wishes in the matter should be considered. Further on there is a curious passage where it is stated that first marriage vows and marriages are to be observed and not set aside in order to remarry, unless, we are told, they have already been annulled by adultery.

THE CULDEES[5]

The rigorous life-style of the early Irish monks was a little too much for human nature and much laxity crept in eventually. Besides, it can never be repeated often enough that they never succeeded in their most fervent and rigorous years in changing the marital and sexual freedoms granted through the brehon laws.

In fact, the secular practices of the Irish of the time began to be accepted in many monasteries. To begin with, the lack of any central political authority was reflected in the Church. Each monastery was absorbed in the little kingdom in which it found itself and the abbacy became hereditary in a manner quite similar to the chieftainship or kingship. We find the distinction between a bishop and an abbot becomes blurred and the abbot is the *comarba* or heir of the founder of the monastery. By the eighth century many abbots and bishops were married men or laymen. The brehon laws have pertinent information on the situation and the following grading of ecclesiastics for legal purposes is illuminating:[6]

i) A virgin bishop has the highest honour-price. For example, seven female slaves must be paid for sick maintenance and *éraic*, if anyone wounds him.

ii) A virgin priest has a price of one slave less.

iii) A bishop of one wife has two-thirds of the price of the virgin bishop and similarly with the priest of one wife.

This speaks for itself and no further comment on it is necessary.

However, the more ascetic spirits in the Church did not accept this situation without demur. In the ninth century an anchoritic movement began which had its origins in the monastery of Tallaght which is known as the Culdee movement. The word 'Culdee' is derived from *céile Dé* (partner of God). The Culdees practised the usual extreme form of asceticism which always found favour in the old Irish Church. It appears that the movement spread successfully in the south of Ireland and we hear of Culdee abbots being appointed in some monasteries here and there throughout the country.

A penitential survives which stems from the Culdees. This gives some inkling as to the severity with which the deeds which were considered sinful could be punished. From the point of view of the subject of this book it should be observed that novices, monks, priests, and nuns are not expelled for sexual 'offences' but merely put to penance. In the case of a bishop, deprivation of his rank is ordered for sleeping with a woman.[7]

In the Culdee penitential there is a general survey of adultery, fornication, sodomy, and masturbation for which the author goes on to prescribe the usual rigorous penances. Then there are certain penances for offences by women specifically. Here are some of the more noteworthy ones:

i) No woman is allowed to receive the sacrament during her menstrual period. If she has intercourse during this time, she gets twenty nights' penance.

ii) Abortion is then mentioned. If the foetus is 'established', there is three and a half years penance for aborting it. This is increased to seven years if the flesh of the unborn child is formed. Fourteen years penance are decreed for an abortion in the case of a foetus 'if the soul has entered it'. If the woman dies as a result of her abortion, a fine of fourteen *cumals* or female-slaves must be paid as the price of her soul. This, it should be recalled, is a double *éraic*.

iii) Penances for 'keening women': 'keeners' were those who mourned the dead at the wake for a fee. This custom has lasted down almost to this day in Ireland. A married woman or a penitent nun was sentenced to fifty nights of penance for keening. If she keened a married woman, a penitent nun, or a woman who died in childbirth, her penance was forty nights. Twenty nights was the penance for keening a lay cleric – a secular ecclesiastic. For keening a king, a confessor, a bishop or a ruler, her penance was reduced to fifteen nights.

The reason for the penalties for keening was probably due to the full-blooded scenes and fun which went on at wakes. Irish wakes in the last century were severely condemned by the Catholic clergy and must have been even more hectic in the time of the Culdees. Evidently, the keening woman had a key-part to play in it all.

There is a story extant regarding a Culdee which is worth retelling. It appears that some Culdees put their virtue to the test after their rigorous austerities by lying in bed with women and trying themselves in this rather odd fashion. How common this custom was, we do not know.

A hermit named Scoithin lived with two beautiful ladies. We hear that they had 'pointed breasts' and Scoithin used these comely lassies to torture himself and suffer what an old text calls 'the white martyrdom'. We also hear that when he became aroused by the proximity of the girls, he betook himself to a tub of cold water to cool his ardour. Naturally, we do not hear what the two ladies thought of all this, but they must have had quite a sense of humour or had small interest in men as lovers. Scoithin was visited by one Brendan, another hermit, who was curious about the mode of life of Scoithin. When he went to bed on the night of his visit, he was promptly joined by the girls. They informed him that this is what they did every night. Poor Brendan found it rather trying to sleep in such arousing company and one of the girls remarked to him: 'This is imperfect, cleric! The man who sleeps with us every night feels nothing at all!' This was poor comfort for Brendan and they next solemnly advised him to go out and immerse himself in the tub of water to dampen his ardours. This, they confided to him, happened also to Scoithin occasionally. By this time Brendan had had enough of this masochism and he remarked that it was wrong for him to carry out this bed-test because Scoithin was a better man than he. He then acted as nature prompted and we hear that both himself and the ladies parted *feliciter* (happily).

The Culdee movement failed in its ultimate object – the total reformation of the Church in Ireland. They had no permanent effect on the brehon laws nor did they reform the monasteries. Indeed, from the beginning of the ninth century onwards the situation became worse from an ascetic's point of view. The raids of the Vikings made a radical change.

CUIRITHIR AND LIADAIN[8]

One of the most famous love-poems from ancient Ireland is probably that composed by Liadain. The circumstances are a little obscure but the story is clear in outline: both loved each other; Liadain took the nun's veil and Cuirithir departed from Ireland.

Liadain was a woman-poet from Kerry and she went on a poet's visit to Connacht. Here she met Cuirithir who entertained her suitably to an ale-feast. He was so attracted to the lady from Kerry that he simply said: 'Why don't we unite? A son or ours would be fine!' This request was turned down by Liadain who pointed out that she was on a poet's tour and marriage would destroy it. She proposed to him that he visit her at her home.

In due course Cuirithir set out for Munster with one servant. He wore a bad cloak on his journey while his servant carried a good one in a leather bag together with spear-tops and the usual books which people like Cuirithir would carry about with them. When he came to Liadain's homestead, he stopped at the well, dressed himself in his purple cloak, set his spear-heads on handles and began to brandish them. Here was approached by a fellow named Mac Dá Cherda, who is described as chief poet of Ireland and fool (!) of Ireland, and one who could walk on land and sea with dry feet. Mac Dá Cherda asked Cuirithir whether he was the occupier of the homestead. After some evasive dialogue Cuirithir asked his new acquaintance to go into the house and ask the lady to come to the well to meet him.

The poet enters the house and finds the lady sitting on a couch with four companions. In rather elliptical language he informs her that she is awaited by Cuirithir. In his poetic address to her Mac Dá Cherda says: 'There's not

78

under a veil/A woman with more sense'. Apparently she had taken the veil and vowed herself to chastity. Cuirithir's journey seemed to be in vain.

To seek a solution to this predicament – her promise of marriage and her hasty vow before he came to claim her – both of them travelled on the following day to Cummean, the ascetic monk and writer of a penitential, and sought spiritual direction from him. The word for this relationship in Gaelic is *anmchairde* (soul-friendship), a neat parallel with words such as *cairdes sliasait* (thigh friendship, i.e., sexual activity) and *lámchairdes* (mutual friendship, i.e., masturbation)! He inquires whether they wish for opportunities to speak together or just to see one another! Cuirithir chose the former. Liadain is enclosed in a nun's cell and has limitless opportunities to speak with her loved one. They hold long dialogues in verse and then the monk tells them that they may sleep together with a third person between them.

After this cruel test Cuirithir left and went to the Déise country (the present County Waterford and South Tipperary, the native area of Mac Dá Cherda), where he travelled as a pilgrim. The wretched Liadain followed him but when he heard that she was coming, he took a ship overseas to escape her. Her love-poem is full of the heartbreak of one who has hurt her loved one and has driven him far from her:

> Without joy
> Is that which I have done;
> He whom I've loved, I've hurt.
>
> 'Twas madness
> That his pleasure wasn't done
> For fear of Heaven's King.
>
> Not his loss
> The way that he journeyed
> Through pain into Paradise.

Of small worth
What hurt Cuirithir in me;
To him I was greatly gentle.

I'm Liadain!
I've loved Curithir;
To him I was greatly gentle.

I'm Liadain!
I've loved Curithir;
'Tis as true as reported.

A short while
I was in Curithir's company;
Well did I know him.

The music of woods
Sang to me when with Curithir;
With the murmur of the purple ocean.

'Tis my wish
That Cuirithir be not vexed with me
In spite of all that I've done.

I won't hide it!
He was my heart's love;
Whoever I have loved before.

A fire's roar
Had burned up my heart;
For sure I can't be without him.

We are told that Liadain died of grief for her exiled loved one.

EUROPEAN REFORM

The Christian Church in Ireland went along its own way throughout the Viking troubles without conforming in practice to the rule of the Church in Europe. Married abbots and bishops was the normal thing. For example, one of the scribes of *The Book of the Dun Cow* – one of the most important compendia of Irish tradition from ancient times – was grandson of the head of the Culdees and great-grandson of another ecclesiastic. The abbess of Killeevy convent, Moninne, who died in 1077, was daughter of an abbot and wife of a kinglet herself. All this was not considered something shameful and disreputable but the correct manner of living. To convince the Irish of sin and shame where matters of this kind were concerned, it needed the efforts of clerics from outside and their collaborators in Ireland.

In 1101 a synod was held in Cashel to reform the Irish Church. In the Canon on Marriage the clerics wisely refrained from attacking the customs of divorce and concubinage followed by the Irish. Instead of this they condemned the right to marry step-mother, step-grandmother, sister, daughter, brother's wife or anyone of similar degree of kindred. This throws a rather lurid light on the sex-life of some of the Irish at that time. In addition celibacy was decreed as necessary for an abbot.

In the twelfth century the Norman prelates in England were taking an interest in the Church in their neighbouring island. They saw the brehon law marriages as fornication and attempted to get Irish authorities to change this. The principal reformer of the twelfth century was Maelmaedóc, one of the few canonised Irish saints, who considered the abbots of Armagh an evil and adulterous generation. He spent his life fighting against the independence of the Irish Church and died abroad. When the Normans invaded Ireland in 1169 and afterwards, their king, Henry II, had a Papal Bull permitting him to do this and instructing him to bring the Irish people to the True Faith. This Henry was the same man who had Thomas à Beckett, Archbishop of Canterbury, murdered because of his independence. It should be pointed out that Maelmaedóc and his like who represented the Irish rulers and their laws as sinful all died in their beds. The coming of the Normans saw the end of the hegemony of the brehon laws in Ireland. They were observed in parts of Ireland until the seventeenth century wherever the English government and its servants did not rule.

The end of the twelfth century is, nevertheless, the last time when the liberality of the brehon laws with regard to the supremely intimate matters of marriage and sex was available to the vast majority of the Irish people.

GIRALDUS CAMBRENSIS

To conclude this chapter attention should be paid to the Welsh cleric, Gerald Barry, usually known as Giraldus Cambrensis. This man visited Ireland in the early years of the Norman Invasion and wrote of the country as he saw it. He also described the Irish of the time in a manner somewhat unflattering and has been regarded as a biased writer who relied too much on hearsay and his own imagination. Nevertheless, it is worthwhile looking at some of the things he said on the subject of this book.

Cambrensis saw the Irish people as 'A most dirty people, bound by vices; a people most ignorant of the faith beyond all other nations'. He goes on to say that 'they never contract marriage; do not avoid incest' and adds 'what is most hateful, and contrary not only to faith but to any kind of virtue, is that brothers lead, or I should say, degrade, their brothers' wives into cohabitation'. He expands this further by saying that 'they more truly seduce them, while incestuously knowing them'.[9]

It is surprising to hear this man point out that the clergy were chaste but he explains that they spent nights in drunkenness after a virtuous day spent in the service of God. He expresses amazement that where wine reigns, Venus does not rule and calls it a miracle![10] One wonders whether here we are reading of the new monastic foundations carried out after the time of Maelmaedóc and the reforms introduced into the lives of the secular clergy. It should be remembered that Giraldus went only where his fellow-invaders travelled.

Giraldus makes a wholesale condemnation of the Irish people in his remarks on the amount of bodily infirmities which he says he found. 'We have not seen,' he tells us, 'such a number of people born blind, deaf, crippled in body, or deprived of nature's gifts in any other nation. Of those who are well, there are none better; of those who are badly endowed, there are none worse.' He then goes on to his conclusion: 'It must not be wondered at that a people who are adulterous, incestuous, born and conceived illegitimately, a people who are outside the law, should produce such unnatural types, who shamefully adulterate nature in a hateful and disgusting manner.'[11]

CONCLUSION

WHEN DEALING WITH THE period of Irish history from the beginning of written records until the Norman Invasion, one is constantly frustrated by the scarcity and unreliability of written records. The brehon laws, fortunately, are extant and reliable in their way. They are, however, like all laws, an expression of the ideals to which the society was tending or was supposed to tend. Nevertheless, the whole attitude of these laws towards marital and sexual matters is rather liberal and one thing is clear: women were not mere chattels but had a framework within which they could carve out much freedom for themselves, if they wished. It cannot be stressed too often, however, that the structure of early Irish society was familial and one's freedom was limited to this extent. This applied both to men and women.

From reading the literature of the period under discussion it is interesting to notice that hardly any overt 'sexual' literature is found.[1] By this we mean descriptions in any detail of sexual acts and so forth. The reader learns that such a fellow slept with such a girl or that one girl or man proposed to another that they should make love. The directness of some of these statements in the old stories contrasts with the reticence found in what may be described as intimate details. Those who consider the D. H. Lawrence type of frankness unhealthy and indicative of impotence or the fear of it, may point to this reticence as the normal reaction in a virile healthy society.

On the other hand we should not forget that the stories we have from these ancient times were all copied in monasteries by monks. Against this may be urged the fact that the monks themselves were all too often healthy men with healthy appetites for pleasure of all kinds. It might strike the reader that the absence of downright bawdiness and frankness in intimate details may just be an example of good taste and the desire for privacy. No one may have been interested in this kind of thing.

Another interesting matter is the avoidance of the human figure to a large extent in early Irish art. Much care and love was devoted to abstract design which mirrors the tortuous and fantastic minds of the artists. The absence of nudity is remarkable. Again one might say that the monks are at fault here.

There is one phenomenon which may form a remarkable exception to what has been stated in the foregoing paragraph and that is the 'Sheela-na-gig'. A Sheela-na-gig is a carving of a female which often shows her in a pose where she is enjoying sexual pleasure. It has never been satisfactorily explained to what century these carvings belong. Some favour the era under discussion here, others a later date.[2] It appears to the present writer that all the sheelas which he has seen are later insertions in their present locations, very often the walls of churches! What was the purpose of these frank pictures? One recalls a sheela which shows a lady with fetching breasts, legs splayed out wide, engaging in masturbation. Her sexual organs can be seen clearly. There is no coyness nor reticence. Are we in the presence of a rude folk art? Is this something which mirrors a folk tradition which was kept out of the manuscripts? After all, the manuscripts were for monks and aristocrats who may have wished to avoid any display of common taste, such as this, in print. Some of the sheelas have their ribs displayed and are cadaverous specimens of womanhood. It has been suggested that we have here an illustration of a death-in-life attitude, where the upper part of the figure may mirror mortality and the lower half the source of further life, not to mention pleasure. It is quite a contrast to find in the same area the clothed figure of Christ on a cross, as on the rock of Cashel, and a most explicit and naked pleasure-woman represented on the wall of a church within the old cathedral on the rock of Cashel, although it is not so explicit as the one described above.

It is generally said that these sheela-na-gigs are fertility symbols. The author was assured by an old man, who lived in the vicinity of one of these, that they were pagan pictures. So much for folklore, which may just be right in this case. At any rate, it is out of joint with any attitude of the Christian Church to such matters. Irish society is slow to change nowadays but in early Ireland it must have changed very little and very, very slowly. Thus it could happen that Christianity formed a thin film over pre-Christian thought. It seems quite clear that this is what happened.

Professor T. F. O'Rahilly pointed out that the gods of the pre-Christian Irish underwent euhemerisation at the hands of the monastic scribes.[3] One outstanding example of this was the inclusion of the Irish deities in Irish history as the Tuatha Dé Danann. Sometimes it is not difficult to detect the traces of the ancient gods in the stories. Who, for example, was the goddess of fertility? We may be inclined to say that Queen Maeve of Connacht is one, if the whole Ulster Cycle of tales be taken as mythology without a scrap of historical truth within them. With greater justice Macha may be chosen for that role. A story of how Macha ran a race against horses when near her confinement has already been told. This lady was said to have visited a nobleman who was a widower, attended to the household duties and then did a ritual right-hand turn before going to bed. She slept with him that night and became pregnant. Not only did she become fruitful, but all his land and herds shared the same blessing while she was with him. The prelude to the race against the horses was her admonition to him to avoid telling her name at the great assembly of the Ulstermen to which they went. He broke his promise to her and boasted that she could outrun the royal horses. This led to the fatal race.

Another Macha is said to have ruled Ireland alone, although opposed by two male rivals. She married one but the five grown sons of the other still opposed her. One day she met them and enticed each into a thicket to make love with her. They ended up bound and tied in the thicket and were brought away as slaves to build a royal palace for her.

The lady Anu is described by Cormac Mac Cullenan as *mater deorum hibernensium* (the mother of the Irish gods).[4] He lived in the ninth century and his evidence is to be taken seriously. According to another source the province of Munster was dedicated to Anu and depended on her for its wealth and fertility in man and beast and crops. The twin-peaked mountain in Kerry – the Paps of Dana – are named after this goddess. It is also suggested that holy wells dedicated to Saint Anne in Ireland were originally dedicated to Anu.

With regard to fertility rites it should be stated that some people regard the Sheela-na-gig carvings as survivals of such ceremonies. One author speaks of the popular entertainers in ancient Ireland – the *crossán* – and quotes a triad which mentions the three distinguishing marks of a *crossán*; distended mouth, distended stomach and distended penis. He points out that this could well refer to the Sheela-na-gig, although the carvings are distinctly feminine. Evidently he envisaged the addition of an extra organ to the female figure. Buffoons have always used sex as their chief subject for humour and the *crossáin* may well have formed part of some fertility cult in pre-Christian and early Christian Ireland.[5]

One might conclude with a reference to a famous poem from the period which is spoken of here. It is the poem connected with the *Caillech Béara* – the Nun or Hag of Béara.[6] *Caillach* meant 'veiled one' and this applied both to hag and nun. In the version of the poem here, we read of the old woman regretting the passing of her youth and recalling the fun she had then. She says:

> These are thin and boney
> Since my arms grew slim;
> 'Twas joyous when they acted –
> They were around fine kings.

> Since my arms grew slim,
> They are thin and boney;
> They're not fit to support
> The weight of nice children.

> I don't hold sweet converse;
> Ewes aren't killed for my wedding;
> Slight and grey my hair is;
> A bad veil doesn't make it worse!

She is, or was, a symbol of the goddess of fertility in her youth. Now she has ebbed but, unlike the sea, there is no full tide to be expected. This poem is frankly pagan in its sentiments. There is one stanza where the hag reproaches the young people of a later day for their neglect of love:

> 'Tis riches
> That you love and not people!
> As for us in our lifetime
> 'Twas to people that we gave our love.

The poem stresses the all-important fact that time wears out the vigour and capacity of youth for love. When we think on all the ingenious methods which society has used since these early days in Ireland to rob youth of its joy or to sully it with false guilt, we may well be appalled. We may think of Christ condemning the Pharisees for laying on others heavy and insupportable burdens and not easing them even with the touch of a finger. We may also notice the wrongs done to women and the extremes that have been used in teaching girls and young ladies to accept their burdens as something good and holy. Whatever we think of the old Irish system, we must admit that it endeavoured to give the opportunity to people and above all women to seek their own happiness. After all, life comes but once and, unless we believe in reincarnation, why not make the most we can of it? The Hag of Béara says:

> I've ebbed out but not as the sea;
> Old age has made me mellow.
> Although at this I may grieve,
>
> Shedding my fat was pleasure!

NOTES

INTRODUCTION
1. See *Crith Gabhlach* ed. with notes by D. Binchy, Dublin 1941. Note on *tuath* is p. 109, on *rí* and *rí ruirech* p. 104.
2. See preceeding for *enechlann* and *(corp)-díre pp.* 84–86.
   Similarly *éraic*. It should be mentioned here that all students of the old Irish Laws are deeply indebted to Professor Binchy for his able exposition of the terminology and general import of the brehon laws.
3. See *Ancient Laws of Ireland*, Vol. II, p. 351. It should be stated here that the five volumes of brehon law tracts, although a monumental work, contain many faulty readings and the translations are not always trustworthy. Binchy's work has done much to remedy some of these defects. it should also be noted that Professor Rudolf Thurneysen states in the Foreward to his *A Grammar of Old Irish*, Dublin 1961, p. 15, that many of the brehon law tracts contain language which may be as old as the earliest examples of Gaelic extant.
4. Binchy, pp. 81–82.
5. *Early Irish Law Institutions* by Professor Eoin MacNeill, p. 64f.
6. *Táin Bó Cuailnge* ed. and translated by Cecile O'Rahilly from *Book of Leinster*, Dublin 1967, pp. 1–2.
7. For a different interpretation of this phenomenon see *Éigse*, Vol X, Pt 4, Autumn 1963, pp. 288–99, by Tomás Ó Broin – *What was the debility of the Ulstermen?*
8. *Táin Bó Cuailnge*, p. 32 (Cecile O'Rahilly).
9. See *Three Irish Glossaries*, ed. and trans. by Whitley Stokes, London 1963, p. 36.
10. *Ancient Laws of Ireland*, p. 355.
11. *Foras Feasa ar Éirinn*, Vol VIII (ITS), trans. and edited by P. Dineen, pp. 28–32.
12. *Ancient Laws of Ireland*, Vol. II, p. 355.
13. See *Cáin Adamnáin*, ed. and trans. by Kuno Meyer, Art. 50.
14. Keating, *Foras Feasa ar Éirinn*, pp. 214–6.
15. *Ibid.*, p. 178.
16. *Ibid.*, p. 232.
17. *Ibid.*, p. 314.
18. *Ancient Laws of Ireland*, Vol. V, p. 177.

MARRIAGE
1. See *Lebor na hUidre* (Book of the Dun Cow), ed. by R. I. Best and O. J. Bergin, Dublin 1929. For a version of this story, see p. 307ff.
2. See *Kurzgefasste irische Grammatik* by Ernst Windisch, Leipzig 1880, pp. 118–20.
3. *Ancient Laws of Ireland*, Vol. V, pp. 132–4.

4. *Crith Gablach*, D. Binchy, Dublin 1941, p. 17.
5. *Ibid.*, p. 16.
6. *Ibid.*, p. 13.
7. *Three Irish Glossaries*, ed. by Whitley Stokes, London 1883. See under *gam* (winter) in Cormac's *Glossary*.
8. Mentioned in P. W. Joyce's *A Social History of Ireland*, Vol. II, p. 439.
9. *Ibid.*
10. See *Revue Celtique*, Vol. XIII, p. 37.
11. *Crith Gablach*, p. 5.
12. *Ancient Laws of Ireland*, Vol. II, p. 355.
13. *Ibid.*, Vol. II, p. 349; Vol. III, p. 317.
14. *Ibid.*, Vol. III, pp. 316-7.
15. See *Crith Gablach*, p. 66 (glossary) for *tinchor.*
16. See *Book of Leinster*, f. 190c.
17. *Ancient Laws of Ireland*, Vol. II, p. 351.
18. *Ibid.*
19. *Ibid.*, p. 381-3. However this applied only to the *cétmuinter* wife.
20. *Ibid.*, pp. 357-61.
21. *Ibid.*, Vol. III, pp. 204-6.
22. *Ibid.*, Vol. III, pp. 550-2.
23. *Ibid.*, Vol. I, pp. 269,301.
24. *Ibid.*, Vol. I, p. 195.
25. See note 10 above.
26. *Foras Feasa ar Éirinn* (ITS publication), Vol. II, trans. Dineen, pp. 272-274.
27. *Ibid.*, Vol. III, pp. 50-52.
28. *Ancient Laws of Ireland*, Vol. II, p. 186.
29. *Ibid.*, p. 177.
30. *Ibid.*, p. 151.
31. *Ibid.*, pp. 187-191.
32. *Ibid.*, p. 151.
33. *Ibid.*
34. *Ibid.*, Vol. V, p. 303.

CUCKOLDRY, ADULTERY AND ABDUCTION
1. *Ancient Laws of Ireland*, Vol. III, pp. 310-314.
2. *Ibid.*, p. 312.
3. *Buile Suibhne*, ed. by J. G. O'Keefe, Dublin 1952.
4. *Ancient Laws of Ireland*, Vol. III, p. 533.
5. *Ibid.*, Vol. II, pp. 540-47.
6. *Ibid.*, p. 382.
7. *Ibid.*
8. *Silva Gadelica*, ed. by Standish H. O'Grady, Dublin 1892, pp. 253-6.
9. *Ancient Laws of Ireland*, Vol. III, p. 292.
10. Keating, *Foras Feasa ar Éirinn*, II, pp. 334-6.
11. *Ancient Laws of Ireland*, Vol. V, p. 272.

DIVORCE

1. *Ancient Laws of Ireland*, Vol. V, p. 112.
2. The term used in the laws is not quite clear. It seems possible that it means a mark or a blemish which remains.
3. *Ancient Laws of Ireland*, Vol. V, p. 293.
4. *Ibid.*, Vol. 4, p. 185.
5. *Ibid.*, Vol. III, pp. 315–7.
6. *Ibid.*, Vol. II, p. 363.
7. *Ibid.*, pp. 365–7.
8. *Ibid.*, p. 367.
9. *Ibid.*
10. *Ibid.*, p. 373.
11. *Ibid.*
12. *Ibid.*, pp. 375–7.
13. *Ibid.*, p. 391.
14. *Ibid.*
15. *Ibid.*, p. 397.
16. *Ibid.*, p. 401.
17. *Ibid.*, p. 405.
18. *Ibid.*, p. 407.

AN EXTRAMARITAL ADVENTURE

1. The text of *Serglige Con Chulann* is to be found in *Lebor na hUidre*, ed. by R. I. Best and Osborn Bergin, Dublin 1929. *Tochmarc Etaíne* is found in *Ériu*, Vol. V and edited by Windisch, Bergin and Best.

THE CHRISTIAN CHURCH

1. *The Irish Penitentials* ed. by Ludwig Bieler, Dublin 1963. 'Synodus I S. Patricii' pp. 54–59. In all cases in this chapter, where Bieler is quoted as source of the material used, I am indebted to him for his comments on the age of the material.
2. *Ibid.* See *Penitentiale Vinniani*, pp. 74–95.
3. *Ibid.* See *Penitentiale Columbani*, pp. 96–107.
4. *Ibid.* See *Synodus II S. Patricii*, pp. 184–197.
5. See *The Church in Early Irish Society* by Kathleen Hughes, London 1966, pp. 173ff for Culdees.
6. *Félire Óengusso Céli Dé*, ed. and trans. by Whitley Stokes, London 1905, p. 41.
7. See *Ériu* VII, 1914 for 'An Irish Penitential', ed. E. J. Gwynn, pp. 138–75.
8. *Liadain and Cuirithir* ed. and trans. by Kuno Meyer London 1902.
9. Giraldus Cambrensis – *Opera*, ed. by James F. Dimock, London 1867, Vol. V. p. 164.
10. *Ibid.*, pp. 172–3.
11. *Ibid.*, p. 181.

CONCLUSION

1. One of the most bawdy instances of outspokenness is found in a medieval Gaelic story *Aided Ferghusa* where the story of how the King of Ulster made love to the tiny queen Bebo and afterwards taunted her husband with it is told. This is not found in the period treated in our book. In *Aided Ferghusa* we find the neat commentary on a couple making love four times at the same meeting. (See *Silva* Gadelica, ed. by Standish O'Grady, Dublin 1892, p. 244).

2. 'Irish Sheela-na-gigs' by Edith M. Guest in *Journal of the Royal Society of Antiquities of Ireland*, 1936, Vol. LXVI, pp. 107–129. See also *The Witch on the Wall*, Jørgen Andersen, London 1977.

3. See T. F. O'Rahilly Early *Irish History and Mythology*, Dublin 1946, *passim*.

4. *Three Irish Glossaries*, Whitley Stokes, London 1862, p. 2.

5. See article by M. Ó Seághdha in *Féilscríbhinn Torna* (ed. by S. Pender, Cork 1937) entitled 'Stair an Síla-na-gig', pp. 50–55.

6. See *Ériu* Vol. VII, for 'The Lament of the Nun of Béra' by Osborn Bergin, pp. 240–1 for text used in this chapter. Note that *caillech* meant the 'veiled one' (pallium = *caille*).

INDEX